I am a New Creation

AN AUTOBIOGRAPHY

Uong Nguyen

Ark House Press
PO Box 1321, Mona Vale NSW 1660 Australia
Telephone: +61 2 9007 5376
PO Box 47212, Ponsonby, Auckland New Zealand
Telephone: +64 9 416 8400 | arkhousepress.com
Ark House Press, a division of Initiate Media.

Cataloguing in Publication Data:
Author: Nguyen, Uong
Title: I Am A New Creation
ISBN: 9781921589966 (pbk.)
Subjects: Priests/Australia/Biography/Immigrants/Vietnamese.
Dewey Number: 262.14092

Cover design and layout by initiateagency.com

Endorsements

It was while I was staying with Uong and his family that I had the opportunity to read the draft copy of this book.

After reading a couple of chapters I sat down in his living room across from him and asked, 'Is this story actually true?' Uong smiled and assured me it was.

Like me, when you read Uong Nguyen's riveting story, it will astound you. It's totally miraculous. It tells of unimaginable pain and loss while at the same time proof of the redeeming power of his compassionate God.

Looking at Indochina from afar (even though I had American friends in the Vietnam war) still never gave me any sense at all of what it could have been like being on the receiving end of United States bombers. One of these killed Uong's best friend as they played together at the edge of their village.

A B52 flying at great altitude basically destroyed the mind and ultimately the life of his brother as well.

Many of us will have read stories of the brutality of Pol Pot and the Khmer Rouge in Cambodia savagely murdering two million of their own people. Uong's story of survival tells of being captured and tortured by the Khmer Rouge for two terrible years. The fact that he survived at all while others around him died, is an absolute miracle in itself.

With the intervention of the International Red Cross, eventually Uong was delivered by his captors to Thailand and again this young man was imprisonment in Thai Military Jail and was interrogated by the Thai Intelligent for information that they think he has. Months in Thai Military Prison and from there Uong was sent to a refugee camp and became a refugee and lived there from 1985 to 1989.

But I have to say that the greatest miracle of all was that this man, who grew up in North Vietnam with no concept of the Living God actually called out to an unknown god in the dense and unforgiving jungles of Cambodia and heard him answer.

Years later he arrived in Australia as a refugee and there found God and inspired by the forgiving of the Lord Jesus Christ, who gives Uong the ability to forgive and to know forgiveness.

I commend Uong and his story to you, it is an intense read, but it will impact your life as you find in its pages a new sense of both the degradation of the human condition and the all redeeming grace of God.

David Garratt
New Sound Publishing

....

It is my great privilege to be considered the friend of Uong, and being a brother in Christ has added a dimension to my life I treasure. Twisting Job's words somewhat, I have heard of Uong with the hearing of the ear but now my eyes have seen him. Having picked up snippets of his life story prior to the reading of this work, finally comprehending the enormity of the life of this remarkable gift of God is truly amazing. I commend reflection on this book for spiritual nourishment, development of faith and stimulus to believe God for continued miracles in the daily activity of life even if it never parallels these epic proportions.

Dr. David Parker,
Senior lecturer at Alphacrucis Bible College, Sydney

....

As I read the remarkable *death to life* story of Uong Nguyen,

I could see a life where, while sin and death sought to overwhelm him, Grace was much stronger and ultimately led to the man and leader we know Uong is becoming today!

I have known Uong for almost all of the years he has lived and ministered in and through Jesus Family. I see a profitable life-a life like Joseph where, while all was intended for evil, God meant it and worked it for good!

The account of a frog (sent by God?), who became his friend was part of the restoration of trust in Uong's life.

When asked the question–'How did you survive as a Khmer Rouge captive?', his response was –'I made myself useful!'

Even in deprivation, by Grace Uong managed to be profitable and to add value to others!

This is a 20/21 account of survival and discipleship from which readers will draw much encouragement and inspiration!

Read on and be strengthened in your faith to live a life that adds value to others and the world.

Mark 8 v 36 says, 'What does it profit a man to gain the whole world and lose his soul!'

Max Palmer
Director, Life International Network , New Zealand

I served with the Australian Army in South Vietnam during 1970-71. Had Uong and I met in our previous years, in our military service, the probability is that one of us would have killed the other.

In this book Uong gives an account of his childhood and his unit's ambush and capture by Khmer Rouge soldiers, whilst on a reconnaissance patrol inside Cambodia. He tells of the bewildering reaction and fury of his senior officer following the ambush and his years served as a prisoner of war both in Cambodia and Thailand. He also tells of the brutality and torture suffered at the hands of a 12 year old, to his life in a refugee camp and the mysterious power of a torn Bible, to his arrival and life in Australia. You will be amazed at the events that unfold.

Through this astonishing and moving journey, Uong was in control of nothing except his own state of mind, a personal survival strategy and the desire to return to his family. He wasn't aware that he was watched and loved every step of the way.

The reader will be moved to hope, and trust, for greater things in their own lives.

Trevor King
Australian Vietnam Veteran 1970-71

Contents

Acknowledgments

Foreword

If you were to meet Uong Nguyen today you would have no idea that 25 years ago he was being viciously tortured as a prisoner of the Khmer Rouge.

At first glance no signs of the hurts of the past are evident. His gracious smile and gentle manner are deceptive. You would think they reflect a lifetime of peace and tranquillity without a care in the world. What they do reflect is the amazing healing and restorative power of the gospel of Jesus Christ.

For many months Uong sat in classes I taught at Tabor College and I had no inkling of the struggles he had endured in his youth – torture, exposure to the elements, betrayal, disease, loneliness, squalor, discouragement and hovering more than once on the brink of death – nor of his incredible bravery in the face of unwarranted injustice and malicious cruelty.

Christ had worked a miracle in his life and turned him into a new person.

Of the many extraordinary events in Uong's life, there is one that stands out to me. It is not the most dramatic or the most frightening, but it is remarkable nevertheless. Uong and his mates had torn up two Bibles and used the pages for wallpaper in their hut in a Thai Refugee Camp. One baking, humid day he was lying on his bunk gazing at the wall and found himself reading a passage from the biblical book of Ecclesiastes right there before his eyes – a text that was to have huge consequences for his life. God's miracles are sometimes disarmingly simple.

Today Uong is married and engaged in full-time work as a Christian pastor.

The Bible tells us that Jesus is able to sympathize with our weaknesses because he was in every respect tempted as we are (Hebrews 4:15). In the same way, Uong Nguyen is well able to identify with those who suffer rejection, pain, betrayal and fear because he has experienced it all himself.

This is a book that will grip your attention, move your heart and challenge your will.

I hope you will read every word. In fact, I will be surprised if you don't.

Dr Barry Chant
Founding President Tabor College
Author and Teacher

....

I found Uong Nguyen's story captivating and profound. I was unable to put it down.

It is impossible to fully comprehend both the extent of Uong's suffering and the magnitude of God's mercy and provision.

Uong's sense of journey with God from a very limited understanding to full commitment is an incredible example of human tenacity and God's amazing grace.

Thank you, Uong, for revisiting your suffering and thus allowing me and future readers to have a little window into your inspiring life's journey.

Dr Vanessa Chant
Faculty Head of Counselling
Tabor College, New South Wales

Introduction

When my family and I moved to Cabramatta, in Sydney, Australia in 1988 to pioneer a new church in the most multicultural local government region in the world, we moved out of our comfortable western world into a world that has no borders. Locations like Cabramatta have become home to those who have fled war, torture and discrimination. It is in this world we have seen a church develop that is reaching people from all ethnic backgrounds and social status.

Many of those who have come here have left all to find freedom, yet so many are still caught by their pasts and never find the peace that they are looking for. As we have built a church, which is a genuine family, many have become part of this community and been able to rebuild their lives. This book, 'I am a New Creation,' is the story of one man and his journey from atheism to genuine faith in Christ. The journey of his life is so amazing that you might ask yourself, 'Is it true?' It has been my privilege to have journeyed with Uong, since his arrival in Australia, and I have first hand witnessed the amazing changes in his life.

Uong currently is on the staff at Jesus Family and is active in pastoral ministry, having completed a Bachelor of Ministry at Tabor College. Uong also travels to Vietnam and Cambodia to minister. He has had the privilege to minister to the nation where he previously suffered cruelly at their hands. He has had to face his past and has walked again in the places where he was tortured, this time to minister life to those who were once his enemy.

In reading this book, you may think that Uong has spent many hours in counseling to deal with all the issues in his life. Uong's freedom and new life is the result of the grace of God. The process of change was just that, a process. When Uong first started attending the church he would travel two hours by train to come to the Sunday service and then another two hours home again in the evening; if he fell asleep on the way home he would end up in the holding yards at Newcastle. I had the privilege of leading Uong in the sinner's prayer when he responded to his first altar call; he was the first convert in our fledgling church that was at that time meeting in our home. Uong's life did not change overnight. His weekends consisted of heavy drinking with his ex -soldier friends on Saturday and then coming to church with a hangover on Sunday, where many times he would sleep through the message. Two years after his initial decision to follow Christ, Uong was a different person, the past had truly become the past and Uong was well on his way to being a new creation.

I have travelled with Uong and lived with his family in Vietnam. Also, I have been with him in Cambodia as he ministers and relates with the people there, so have watched him grow in his faith from the very beginning. I have listened to him as he has shared his journey and have seen some of the places that are spoken of in this book.

This story is not only amazing, but it shows the protection of God over our lives. Just as Job was protected, so also was Uong. In the natural he should not have survived; some people call it fate, but I know it was the hand of God.

There are places in the world, where people from the refuge dump of life have found a safe haven and when the grace of God is released in these places trophies of grace can be found. This story is but one of many that can be found in Jesus Family.

David Boyd
Senior Pastor
Jesus Family Centre Cabramatta

Chapter one

MY LIFE BEGINS

---

*T*he Spirit of the Lord is clearly telling me that today, in this
meeting, there is a young man. You have been through a lot.
*You have faced death and much hardship in life. The things you
have endured are beyond imagination.*

*Yes, you have endured so much, and now you have freedom.
Yet you still can't sleep. Constant nightmares keep you up at night.
The problem is you want to keep all these troubles within you.
Your memory has been locked up; it's still overwhelmed by things
from the past. The past still influences you, and your joy has been
stolen. You wish that the passing of time would help to wipe away
your pain! But don't be mistaken: time cannot and will not heal
you. Only the Lord can.*

*What other people did to you—taking away your friends,
betraying your trust—you are an eyewitness to the horror. You
have been imprisoned, enduring physical torture for months on
end, along with emotional abuse and more. Often you felt you were
lost.*

*The Lord clearly wants to say to you: "Today is your time." You
need to come to him and surrender your life totally; trust in Him
with all your heart. Take Him as your peace and He will heal you.
He will restore you. The Lord's hand has been on your life and you
haven't even recognized it. He is the one who rescued you from the
pit—not luck. He is the one who brought you here and arranged
everything for you. No one else, my friend.*

Come to him. Don't argue or stop and wonder. Trust Him. Then you will find the way, you will know peace, you will see the light for your life.

Open up, be humble and share with the Lord your God, for He knows who you are and what you have been through. Regain some trust so that you may share with others all the pain and suffering you have suppressed. Find trust again and enjoy life!

You are in God's hands. You cannot run away forever. Come, accept Him, submit yourself to Him, commit your life to His care and serve Him only. Come, I want to pray for you today.

The man spoke with such confidence, as though he had been talking with me as an acquaintance for a long time and clearly knew my past. His finger was drilling the air as he spoke, and there was a genuine look of deep care and concern in his eyes.

I sat motionless among my new friends in the small, newly established church. There were only about a dozen people there. Some had been Christians for years, some only a few weeks. I was bemused, even stunned, by the speaker's words. At first I looked around to see whether he was speaking to somebody else, but no one looked the part. Then in my heart, and with conviction, I knew the preacher was speaking directly to me.

As an ex-atheist I was raised in doubt. The pain of the past had taught me not to trust or rely on anyone. Even though I had recently become a believer in Christ, my past still held me. At that moment, I didn't know that his words were a revelation from God since I had never heard about the gift of prophecy. Hearing him speak about my life with such confidence and accuracy made me even more puzzled.

But being amazed is totally different to being convicted, let alone responding to someone's concern. Without reason, I hurriedly left the house while the meeting drew to a close. I went to the back garden where I squatted among the vegetables.

A few minutes later, I was interrupted by one of the young women. "I think that word was about you," she said. "If he was speaking about your life, then God must want to do something."

I looked up shyly, hesitantly, but didn't answer a word.

The friend who had brought me to church soon came out as well. We'd been friends for some time. "What do you think about what was said in the meeting?" she asked.

I looked at her bewildered. "I think he was speaking about me. Did you tell him my story? Is that how he knew?"

She looked at me, her eyes filled with compassion and self-control. "No, I didn't speak to him. Even though I know him personally, I honestly haven't shared anything about you with him. It's God who revealed it to him by His Spirit. You've never told me anything about your life anyway, so how could I tell him?"

"So do you think what he said in the meeting is a genuine prediction?" I asked.

"No, not a prediction." She shook her head trying to find the words to correct my confusion. "It's a revelation."

"I don't know about revelation, but what he said, and the way he looked at me, it seemed like he intended to talk about me. Right?"

"Yes," she nodded.

"Certainly," the other lady confirmed.

"So what can I do?"

"Just come back inside and be open to God. Let the man pray for you. You have nothing to lose and everything to gain."

We went back into the house. The speaker was talking and laughing with others in the small kitchen. He had a cup of hot coffee in his hand. My friend had more confidence with him than I did and approached him directly.

"Can I introduce my friend to you?" she asked. "That prophetic word during the service was about him. Can you pray for him?"

"Of course," the man consented. He put his cup down on the table, took a few steps towards me, and put out his bony hand to shake mine. The gesture eased the tension.

"Ah, it's you," he laughed. "Yes, I want to talk to you. My name's Peter Morrow and I'm from New Zealand."

He smiled and I felt immediate trust.

"Now, young man, during the preaching, I felt like the Lord wanted to speak to you. I saw a picture of your life in prison. I saw you were chained under a tree, being tortured. The picture was very dark. I saw you surrounded by a pack of beasts; they were attacking you from every side. Your mouth was open, gasping for air. I saw you cry to the Lord for help. Is that true?"

"Yes, it's true," I whispered, and suddenly I felt a strong sense of conviction. I knew then what I needed. "Can you please pray for me?"

"Absolutely! Do you mind if I place my hands on you?"

"It's OK." I raised my hands in a simple gesture, humble like a child willing to accept something new.

As he placed his hands gently on my arm, everyone else in the house suddenly stopped talking and silently began praying too. It was a simple prayer, short and to the point.

When did my life begin to change? I don't know the exact time, but it was in this meeting that I received the remarkable touch from God that became the turning point in my life.

Chapter two

A CHILDHOOD IN PAIN

No one ever totally forgets their childhood memories. The things that happened in my childhood eventually affected the way I thought about the world. Only when I finally responded to the salvation offered by Christ and received a new life in Him did I begin to build a brand new life.

Memories of my early childhood are vivid and full of strife. I was a boy at a time when my nation, North Vietnam, was at war. We were still recovering from the long struggle for independence from French colonization, and now we were fighting South Vietnam. Revolution and war had wrought much damage on our society.

I was born in 1962, the third youngest of a large family of nine. In those days, life in Ha Tay (now Hanoi) was very hard. My father, Quyen, was forced to abandon his teaching post after the victory over the French in 1954 because he was out of the Communist government's favor. War creates many victims, and the post-war period, when regimes and governments change, creates more. It was not easy for my father in those days, and of course this affected our family. If Dad had not had the inner strength and courage to live for his family, we, his children, would have been worse off. Now, when I think about Dad, I realize I owe a lot to his tenacity in life and commitment to his family.

Dad was once an ardent nationalist. He devoted all his time, intellect and energy to help fight for the independence of the nation. The irony was, when the political purpose was achieved, he was dumped on the premise that he belonged to the professional class. The new government desired a brand new social structure that could go along with the Marxist-Leninist ideal. It wanted everything new: a different leadership style only a little short of the Maoist ideal of poor, uneducated farmers ruling the country. Dad belonged to the old school so he could not be trusted with anything by the new government.

If a job is a man's security, a profession his identity, and position his pride, then Dad was denied all three. He had a quiet, thoughtful, and sometimes tricky personality, yet he hardly spoke about his past life. Maybe he knew that living under the watchful eyes of the Communist regime was dangerous, so the safest thing to do was to keep your head down, mind your own business, and pretend you knew less. This allowed you to live a life without harassment in the new 'peaceful' era. Or perhaps he was truly at peace with himself. I could never tell because he never shared. "I don't have much to say," he commented whenever we asked about his past. What else could he say when the whole of North Vietnam was under the control of the Communists?

In the 1950s and '60s, when the Communists had all the advantage, the ideal society was deemed to be centered in the Soviet Union, the Eastern Bloc or China. It was the time when Communist ideology flourished and the normal citizen in those nations was drowning in the wave of that movement. At the same time, Vietnam had recently won independence from the French and was still at war with itself. The USA's involvement in that struggle seemed to keep increasing also, which tended to escalate the local commitment to total war.

National establishment, the hope of rebuilding the country from a long war, and national security were the top priorities for the new regime. These political elements became an effective tool for the Communist propagandists. In North Vietnamese society, if there was any sign of dissidence towards that mechanism, it would be labeled 'counter-revolutionary' and crushed without mercy. So Dad had to swallow his pride for the sake of his young family, as any man devoted to his family would do. Dad could never throw away his wife and children for position because we were so valuable to him.

Dad also came from a strong tradition of conservative Confucianism in Vietnam, where family and nationhood were regarded as more important than self. Many scholars in the West were influenced by Judeo-Christian ethics and so had principles of spirituality that allowed them to withstand the advance of Communism. Dad was influenced by *Tam Giáo*, a blending of the ideal society of Confucianism, the mysticism of Tao and the fatality of self-denial in Buddhism. He could do little against Communism. At first he welcomed the teaching of Communism's idealistic society, but it cost him his job and more than half of his life living under the repression of that bizarre philosophical experiment.

In my early childhood, I can remember that we were very poor, almost destitute. Dad had lost everything, and after he served his enforced prison term he returned to us, and then had to leave his ancestral home and move elsewhere. He was allowed to build his new house on his older brother's estate. At the age of three, I did not want to give up my old home. "I don't want to leave! I want live here in the old house!" I yelled, grabbing anything—a pole, a door knob, a banana tree—to prevent anyone taking me away. Stubborn as I was, I fought hard to remain in the old house, but in vain. It was my cousin Cuong who overpowered me and carried me to the new home.

The village lifestyle was very tight and closely knit. It was a community and often consisted of connections between relatives. We considered many cousins to be more like siblings. Cousin Cương, who later died in the war, was so close that I thought he was my eldest brother. He was an exceptionally good teacher, but he was born into a different generation. He was very sympathetic towards my father and for that reason wanted to give Dad a helping hand. He helped us to study and do our homework, and encouraged us to pursue an education.

Dad was a major intellectual influence in our lives. But it was Mum who inspired us with love and practical living. I loved her dearly, and I frequently thought about how to repay her when she got old. I often told my siblings, "You can study well and all go out and achieve great things in the world, but as for me, I will stay home. I will be a farmer, work in the garden and on the farm, and I will take care of Mum and Dad when they are old." That was my promise to my parents when I was a very young age. My parents still remind me of what I said today, even though I am no longer a Vietnamese citizen, and it hurts that I cannot fulfill it.

Meal times were the most important times in our family, especially the evening meal. We ate under a kerosene light and shared our food in equal portions. This was the time when Dad often chose to share something with us. He would speak of someone's mistake that we needed to take notice of, or of some bad behavior he needed to discipline. But often in those meal times, Dad told us about values and standards, the principles of a good work ethic and the way of living in a family. He emphasized the relationship between children and other people in society. In this way, I learnt my social skills from both my parents.

Dad had been a poet and a very good teacher. He told us many stories, and his great humor often turned an ordinary story into a great one, full of fun and completely captivating. His voice was always very animated. Most of his stories were drawn from great heroes of the past and present. He told parables, made up riddles, wrote poems and related legends and myths both from the East and the West. But the majority of stories he drew from Vietnamese history and ancient China. We loved to hear them all, and when the rain came between seasons we had plenty of time to listen.

Another outstanding thing I recall about my family was how Mum and Dad agreed with each other. They did not fight between themselves. Therefore in our family, even though we were very large and poor, we functioned very well, in an orderly manner. Dad often told us, "I may be useless to this government, but I will never be a useless person to my children." We were truly proud of him.

From the age of six to ten, a lot of changes happened around me. In 1967 Cuong left his teaching post to join the army. Three of my sisters got married and moved far away from home with their husbands, who were also serving in the army. Tru, my eldest brother, won a national award and was allowed to enter the National University in Hanoi at the age of 15. I had never seen Dad respond to news like he did to that. He was so joyful when he held the letter informing Tru of his award. Indeed, Tru's entrance to the university was the first from the village in his generation. It surprised even the local Communist party member, for he was a pure farmer of several generations and very insecure. Full of jealousy, he did not like anyone in the village to be that successful. Dad, however, threw a big party to show off Tru's achievement, as was the tradition in Vietnamese families who had a son enter that prestigious university. Many of my father's old friends were invited and his old teacher, Mr Cẩn, whom we all admired and adored, also came.

During that time, Tam, another older brother, also left home, seeking education in a high school with another sister. With so many people leaving home in a very short period, I was affected emotionally. From a family crowded with many people, suddenly more than half had left. The house seemed so empty, especially at dinnertime. "We are so lonely, Mother!" I lamented tearfully. "I don't want to live here anymore. I want to leave too!"

I was too young to understand the political milieu of those days, too young to understand the troubles of politics and war. In the late '60s, North Vietnam was badly affected by the escalation of war and aerial bombardments. Most factories and academic facilities were relocated from the center of Hanoi to rural areas to be among the people. It was an old strategy to empty the city and avoid a major blow from bombing, so the people from Hanoi also evacuated with their jobs. My village became host to the Foreign Language Department of Hanoi National University, and the students came to live with the people in the village while learning English. At the same time many soldiers in their green uniforms also came to take refuge in the village. As kids we liked to imitate their training and fighting skills. They were innocent games then.

My extended family was host to Mr and Mrs Lieu, who were English teachers. They had three children. Mr Lieu came from Hanoi and had been educated in England but had returned to Vietnam to teach English. He was very aloof and we could never get close to him. He talked to Dad and my uncles, but he ignored us. It was as if we did not exist. We did not like him much, but his wife was a very warm-hearted person.

War brought his family to my village and they lived in my uncle's estate, which was next door. Mr Lieu had a motor bike; we kids had no idea what brand, but we called it *bình bịch* after the noise it made. Anything with an engine was rare in our rural area, so whenever we heard the noise from afar, we knew that Mr Lieu was coming home and shouted, *"Bình bịch về làng!* (The motorcycle is coming home!)" With bare feet, we would run after him despite the brown dust from the village road flying up at us. I don't know whether he enjoyed this attention or if it annoyed him. We didn't care—the sound of the engine attracted us and we liked to have fun. When Mr Lieu was not watching, we would often stuff clay into the muffler to see if he could start the engine. We had a lot more fun when he failed to recognize the bike's problem and became very angry as a result.

The English classroom was made from thatched bamboo. It was situated under the thick shade of the bamboo grove and was half underground. We knew nothing about the art of camouflage and we would often laugh at the building, describing it as a 'pig house'. But we enjoyed playing in the classroom whenever there were no students there. I liked to collect the chalk they left behind so I could draw or write on hard surfaces.

The Lieus allowed their children to play with us in the village. Thao, Viet and Quan were good children and outstanding in their behavior. We were friends until the English faculty was ordered to move to another unidentified area. That was the last we ever saw of them.

Chapter three

EARLY SCHOOL DAYS

From 1967 on, the bombing raids in North Vietnam increased in intensity. As young children, we often had to go to the relative safety of the school buildings in our village, or to the next village where the schools were built in trenches. The landscape was beautiful, but we hardly enjoyed it. From Years 1 to 3 we went to school, inseparable from three objects: a bag for textbooks, a large straw hat, and a First Aid Kit.

"You must have all of these to be allowed into the classroom," Miss Vui, our primary school teacher, told us. So every time we went to school, we put our textbooks and note pads into the right hand side of our bag. The First Aid Kit, with a big red cross on it, was full of cotton bandages and red sterile liquid; this was placed in the left side of our bag. On our back we wore a large hat made from rice straw. This was thought to help us avoid being wounded by cluster bomb shrapnel, which was common in the many raids.

Our classroom was taken from the old temple, or *Dinh*, which was the communal meeting place in the middle of the village. Under the new Communist regime all the old things had to be cleared away. So the *Dinh*, a place of worship for our national heroes, was reallocated as a school for us. We could still see many idols and artifacts dumped in a corner of the *Dinh*'s garden, while many stones or poles had been removed to be used as bridges across the water canals.

Miss Vui, my first teacher, was full of goodness and humor. We adored her like a goddess. She taught us simple mathematics and Vietnamese, and, of course, there were plenty of nationalistic songs. In childish voices we would follow her enthusiastically:

The singing sounds louder than the bomb blasts
It comes from the village and is defiant to the mad Americans.
They can bomb, but they cannot stop our will to go to school.
A bomb blast can never stop the sound of our laughing.
Oh! Let's all go to school!

Dinh are places for national and local heroes, so Miss Vui never missed a chance to show us our heroes. Pointing to their statues standing in the corner, she would proclaim, "They were the ones who withstood the might of our enemies and protected our land." These heroes were deeply rooted in the psyche of Vietnamese culture, but they became a national bondage. We could not do any better or go any further than our heroes. And mostly those heroes were very effective killers.

"This country," Miss Vui would say, pointing towards the map, "has defeated the mighty Chinese armies many times; the Mongol army lost its power here; the French recently; and, of course, we will defeat the imperialistic Americans." All eyes were fixed on the tiny country of Vietnam as she spoke of endless battles and victories won. Children always want to be winners, so when we heard about defeating our enemies, we responded, "Yes, yes! We will send the Americans home in disgrace."

Miss Vui often quoted typical sayings of Ho Chi Minh, whose photo we would bow to each morning before school began. "We would all rather fight and die to liberate our country than be enslaved by foreigners." She also gave us moral applications. "Now you are young you cannot fight, but you can prepare by learning and applying the five precepts of Uncle Ho." She then made us repeat those five precepts in front of his photograph on the wall above us. As we stared respectfully at him, we would parrot, "Love your country, love your people, learn well, act well, be honest, humble and courageous." From a young age, we were effectively indoctrinated into Communist ideology.

Mr Lieu's youngest son, Quan, was the same age as me, though he did not attend the same class in my school. He was a very talented storyteller. "Life in Hanoi," he told us with his eyes wide and animated, "is not dirty like here. There are famous lakes, beautiful houses, great buildings, nice streets, beautiful trees and plenty of good things to eat, like ice cream." We had never tasted ice cream, so it was hard to imagine what it was like, yet he made our mouths water. Quan mentioned the books he read and the bicycle he enjoyed pedaling in the mornings and evenings after school. His storytelling skills made us wonder when the war would end and whether we would ever have peace. Then we would all go to explore Hanoi, the city of heroes.

Other students like Thu, Tai and Thinh were special children because their fathers were from South Vietnam and had been evacuated to the north to avoid persecution. They also had many good stories of their homeland in the south. Sitting under the thick shade of the bamboo trees in the village, we agreed that when there was no war, we would go together to visit the mysterious land to the south. We laughed and cherished those simple dreams.

Not long after Quan and his family left the village, an incident occurred that affected my life for a long time. It was one Autumn day in 1972, before the Christmas bombing raids. The American plan was to bomb North Vietnam into submission to achieve its political goals at the Paris Peace Accords. As young kids, we well knew the sound of fighter jets, which flew over our heads constantly. It was deafening, but it was made worse because those faster-than-sound jets flew so low.

The air raid sirens always informed us in advance to jump into the foxholes or trenches to cover ourselves. But with sirens roaring daily for years, we got used to them and often ignored the warnings. In our young minds we thought, *The Americans will attack Hanoi but will never bomb our village.* We felt we had nothing to fear.

At about two in the afternoon on that Autumn day, the sirens began roaring. I was out in the field under a large banyan tree with my close friend, Tai, hunched over playing marbles in the dirt. Marbles were precious to us and prized possessions. Engrossed in the game, we ignored the sirens as we had done many times previously, confident of our safety. The blaring of the sirens, however, was suddenly cut off by the piercing sound of a fighter jet flying in overhead. In the deafening roar I saw a flash as it dropped its consignment of three bombs onto the mulberry factory near my home. The powerful explosions immediately destroyed half the factory, even though the bombs did not hit right on target. Being so near, the explosions threw us flat onto the ground. Dirt flew over us, and in the chaos a piece of shrapnel pierced Tai's chest. He was killed almost instantly.

I cannot forget the incident. It happened more than 30 years ago, yet the shaking movement of the earth, the noise of the detonations, the devastated factory, the blood running out of Tai's chest, and his pale face stand out so clearly in my mind.

After the initial shock of the bombing, I became very confused. My young mind was wandering, almost gone. I understood nothing, felt nothing. While everybody was busy working to extinguish the fires, care for the wounded, or talk to Tai's parents, I quietly walked home, numb.

When I neared home, I saw further damage from the bombs. The roofs of my home and my uncle's home were destroyed. Trees were uprooted. My mother saw me from a short distance and ran very fast towards me.

"Where have you been?" she demanded. Before I could answer she grabbed my shoulder. "Oh, you foolish boy! Why is there blood on your shirt?"

The pitch of her voice was very high. Only then did I realize I had also been wounded. Shrapnel or dirt had pierced my skin at high speed, but I felt no sensation of pain. The wound was shallow, under the skin, with the foreign objects blocking the blood flow, which was why I had not seen any blood before.

Mum reacted immediately by jumping up and down in the middle of the dirt road. She couldn't cope. In the chaos surrounding us, she called out to my cousins for help. They immediately took me to my uncle, Mr Lao, who had studied Western medicine. After touching my face, he gave his diagnosis: "The shrapnel has only lodged in his cheek bone. It's not that dangerous, but the pieces must be taken out immediately, otherwise they will kill him." So, with the approval of my parents, a swift operation began to take out the objects lodged in my face.

For a ten year-old boy it was appalling. All my limbs were tied to a bamboo bed to prevent me hurting myself while struggling. A large bamboo spoon was placed in my mouth to bite down on. There was no painkiller, so a few of my bigger cousins helped to hold my body down as my uncle operated. The knife he used was a shaving razor, and every time the blade sliced through my flesh, I could feel the fabric of my tissue being cut. My body shook uncontrollably in reaction. The pain was beyond description.

Over the following weeks and months, things were supposed to get better, but they didn't. The grief and emotional suffering was too great for me. I had lost my best friend. I was not emotionally prepared to go through such an experience. It was a shocking loss, and the fear of sudden death shook me to the core. "Where did Tai go?" was my constant, nagging, heartfelt question: "Where on earth did Tai go?" The world seemed so dark, and I did not know what to do with myself.

You may say that Communists do not believe in superstition, but they all do when it comes to times of death or hurt or uncertainty. My parents had great sympathy for Tai's mother. They were afraid that if she saw me around, it would trigger more painful memories of her recently lost son. Indeed, once she ran after me demanding a hug and a kiss. So in order to show their kindness to her, my parents agreed that I should never return to the mulberry factory area. They addressed me during dinner: "From now on, Uong, you cannot go anywhere near that factory." The expressions on their faces showed their seriousness. Their words were like a mandate, and I could not disobey.

What a life at that age, to be without friends! I had now lost most of them. Most of my sisters were far away; Tru and Tam were gone; Quan had moved away with his parents; Tai was dead. And the rest of my companions I was deprived of seeing. No one was left. I had many cousins, but they were different and could not compare with the affection of old friends. My tender heart cried out to connect with someone I had played with for a long time. I could be forced not to go to a place bodily, but my memories of friendship, the terrible noise when the fighter jet zipped down, the explosions and Tai's innocent face turning pale haunted me. All these things often resurfaced in my young mind, like a video tape replaying the events.

Cay Da, the big banyan tree where we had played, still stood tall, only a few hundred meters away. I could see it, but I was not allowed to go and touch it. I could only stand afar off, looking at it, yearning. I missed Tai, and the tree was calling me to that place. I was like a faithful dog that had lost its owner and its home. I was free to walk about the farm, but my soul was chained to memories. I was scared and confused; often I did not know what to do. I had been created to trust, to attach myself to friendship and to laughter, but there seemed no one who could understand the void in my heart.

Today I can say I have been healed from this wounded heart. The Lord God has done a dramatic restoration. Yet nowadays, whenever I go back to visit my family, I still see that tree standing there near the river. Even though it has lost a few big branches, it is a living witness to those terrible times. It reminds me of the past. The picture is of poor but happy villagers and the destruction that occurred. I once took my wife and children there, but they could not feel what I felt. Not far away, near the footpath, Tai's grave is still there to remind me of who I was. My emotions are mixed: thankfulness that I am alive and joy at my subsequent story, but at the same time sadness because the life of a close friend was cut so short.

My parents in those days saw the change in me, but they were naïve and untrained to cope with my dysfunctional behavior. Many nights I could not sleep, or if I did I would wake up in the middle of the night sweating, with my mind whizzing with shadows.

September 1 was a big day for all children in North Vietnam: the opening of school. Many children came with smiles. I entered Year 6, but I wasn't smiling. Under the Communist education system, there was a discipline ground. We were rounded up by a loud whistle and then a drum beat. We lined up to learn who was in which class.

"This group will be in 6B and under the supervision of Mrs Suu," the deputy principal of the school told us. Mrs Suu was short, round-eyed, and outwardly easy looking, but she was very moody. This was to cause great issues for me later on.

In the first quarter of Year 6, I could not concentrate on study. Schooling had been my passion before, but now school became a boring place. I wanted to run away. How could I function properly when I was preoccupied with Tai's death? How could I focus when my mind held the picture of his body and the question of whether I would ever meet him or play marbles with him again? There were no answers.

I took to staring at the blackboard more than listening to the lecturing. Mrs Suu saw my blank stare, and at first she was tolerant and patient. But not for long. She was not trained to deal with my state of mind. Lack of understanding brought her frustration, and she poured that frustration out on me. A number of times she shouted angrily, throwing chalk right at my face to call me back to attention.

"You will be sent home! You will be made to repeat Year 6 if you don't try harder!" she threatened.

I *was* trying, but it seemed the harder I tried, the less I succeeded. I had succumbed to the scenario, the motion, the noise and picture of Tai's death.

My poor parents were called to the school and Mrs Suu lectured them about my failure to participate in classroom activities. I could see the sadness, concern, and disappointment on their faces each time they came home from a meeting with my teacher. Of course, they tried to help me. They cooked better food, showed more affection, and paid more attention. As a son, I respected both my parents, and I respected the teacher. I did not want to displease them. But I just could not pull myself together.

Mum vaguely understood that my problem related to the day the village was bombed, so she tried very hard to help me. If anyone suggested anything to aid my recovery, she would do it. Someone came over to our home and told her, "His soul was lost because of the deadly bomb blasts! Prepare a good meal, and then go to the large tree where the bombs exploded and call his soul back." Behind this was the Taoist idea that the noise of explosions can drive away bad spirits (which is why, on New Year's Eve and other special occasions, Chinese and Vietnamese have firecrackers at their parties). Mum believed the bombing had cast my soul away from my body and decided to take the advice.

She followed the procedure without question. One night I saw her cook a nice big pot of sticky rice and boil an egg. She piled these up in a large rice bowl. Just before dinner, around dark, she took that rice bowl and ran fast out of the house and up the dirt road towards the big tree. She ran hard, screaming loudly, "Oh, Uong! Please come back! Wherever you are, come back to your body!"

She was convinced that by appealing to and appeasing my spirit, there was a good chance I would become normal again. But to me it was rather funny. I heard her calling and spontaneously yelled after her, "I am here! I am at home. Why do you have to call me back?" She gave no answer. Only when I followed her did she say angrily, "Be quiet! You are not here with us anymore! You are not the same! Your soul and your spirit have flown away from us."

"But I *am* here. Why do you keep calling?" I protested.

Mum totally ignored me and persisted with the magic art of bribing the spirit. *Maybe by giving his spirit a good meal it will come back,* she reasoned. That was the animist belief. But what could she really do? At least she tried hard to rescue her son from his strangeness and lostness. Mothers know best what to do with their children when they are sick, and often authority doesn't mean much to them when their children are in danger. She was desperate to save me.

Chapter four

THE RETURN OF MY BROTHER

W orse was yet to come for my family. Tru, my eldest brother, was discharged from Hanoi University not long after the bombing of our village. If before Mum and Dad found joy and satisfaction in him, then his discharge from the university broke their hearts.

The evening Tru came back was unexpected. He carried all his belongings with him. We, the younger ones in the family, were overjoyed when we saw him, but Tru did not return that affection. He had nothing cheerful to say that evening.

Tru had often been the life of the party before. Usually when he came back to visit us on a weekend, he would be by himself and carry few books. He would be cheerful, almost always smiling, as though his dreams had come true. Often he would hold my youngest sister Chin tight and encourage her to jump on him for piggyback rides. But that evening his face was downcast, clearly displaying disappointment and sadness; black rings circled his eyes. He did not even want to say hello to anybody. Somehow, we knew that something unusual had happened.

"Why are you home so late, son?" Mum asked, preparing the evening food.

"Why did you have to bring this heavy box with you?" my father followed.

Tru did not want to give an answer. He sat on a stool at the table, his left hand supporting his miserable face. I saw him fight hard to prevent tears from flowing. He looked up at the ceiling as if to find words there because he did not want to show disrespect to my parents. However, he could say nothing. Suddenly he stood up, walked around and burst into tears, then buried his face in his palms, sobbing hard.

Dinner was always our fun time, when every member of the family would talk and interact with each other. But with the bad news from Tru, the dinner that evening was very somber. Everyone ate their food but nobody spoke. The kerosene light in the middle of the table was very dim; its weak, yellow light reflected and magnified the sadness on the faces of Tru, my parents and my two younger siblings. It was a hard night to forget.

As a young ten year-old boy, I could not understand the whole story when Tru later told my parents about being discharged. The start of his problems was a US bombing raid that targeted his university. The authorities had evacuated the different faculty members and students from Hanoi to Vinh Phu Province, northwest of Hanoi, to protect them, but an unexpected night attack hit the temporary campus. Students in Tru's faculty were asleep when the mighty B52 bombers arrived. All the students, in a confused state, ran to the bomb shelters, but with lethal accuracy the B52s dumped their loads right onto the campus. No bomb shelter could withstand the serial explosions. Tru's shelter was wiped out and then covered with soil. He and a few other students miraculously survived, but many did not. Physically he was alive, but the bombing caused much damage to his young mind.

After the raid, all surviving students were mobilized to help other victims. Tru was not prepared for the carnage of that night. With his feeble torchlight shining, he was confronted with the dead, the spilt blood, the body parts of young men and women scattered all over the campus. He heard the agony and groaning of the wounded. What he saw and experienced that night destroyed his brilliant, young mind forever.

We went to bed with our minds a blur, but around 1.00 am, while everyone was in a deep sleep because of the hard work of the day, Tru suffered an epileptic attack. We heard strange noises and the pounding and shaking of his body, twisting hard; the noise awoke everybody. None of us knew what to do, and it was quite a while before Dad could light the kerosene lamp. Seeing Tru struggling under the mosquito net, we immediately jumped to his side. Everyone held onto his limbs while Dad held his head to prevent it knocking against the hard timber frame.

Tru's epileptic seizures attacked him almost every night, often after midnight. It meant total disruption; no wonder the campus had to discharge him. As he stayed home, his symptoms got worse and he began to suffer attacks even during daytime. This meant that our family had to have a full-time caregiver for him.

All of this was greatly disturbing for me. Already I had trouble concentrating and studying in that difficult Year 6 class. With a troubled mind, loss of sleep and disarray in the family because of Tru, I lost the taste for study completely.

With Tru now sick and staying at home, my poor parents faced tremendous pressure. I could see the stress and sadness on their faces. Their behavior also changed. Dad used to be very self-controlled, calm and always in charge. But witnessing the epileptic attacks on his beloved son, day in and day out, he did not cope well. There were no more fun stories at dinner, no more riddles, no more historical tales. Dad's energy was consumed by his concern for the family's brightest son.

Vietnam was at war, so doctors and most medicines were saved for the worst cases. Tru had no chance of being treated by professionals. My parents, therefore, started to sell whatever they had to buy the various medicines people suggested, hoping that one day their son would return to normal and continue to pursue his dream. They traded treasures, ancestral artifacts, even gifts from both grandparents that had been hidden away for hard cash and good doctors. We looked for both Western-trained doctors and herbal medicine practitioners. But Tru was a kind of black-hole consumer, and my parents' resources were limited. The day came when there were no more things to sell.

Dad had to look for another alternative. He started to practice herbal medicine himself. In those days most Confucian scholars in Vietnam could also function as herbalists if they wanted to. They had the knowledge of plants and they could read the herbalist books written in ancient Vietnamese or Chinese characters. Dad followed the teachings and traveled to the forests and jungles to collect plants, tree roots, seeds, flowers and animal parts. If there were things he could not find, he did manual work for money to buy them.

Dad had to travel very far for weeks on end to find the right ingredients for his medicines. He became more distant and more absent from home. Mum also had to work harder in the collective farm to gain enough points to exchange for rice for the family (every working day a farmer earned ten points, equivalent two or three kilograms of rice with husk). Otherwise we would all have starved to death between the harvests.

Before Dad went away on a journey that he knew would take weeks or months, he would call me aside. "I will go very far, even close to the Chinese border, to look for medicine. Can you be the man of the family?" Dad would look at me intensely and ask me to be responsible in taking care of Tru. "Always be very close to your brother or he will fall into the fire and get burnt, or into the fish pond and drown." Each time he talked like this his eyes grew sad and pained. "Can you do it?" he would ask.

I was no more than ten years old, but I replied to Dad's requests in a positive and cooperative way. This was a family issue, so we worked together to tackle it. It was not just about obedience; it was about family, and I could not simply let my parents endure all the hardships in life because I knew they had endured a lot already.

"Dad, you can go!" I urged him. "I can handle my brother." That was my way of reassuring him, and my father trusted that I was capable of doing the things he asked.

To take care of Tru in the daytime was easy, but nighttime was a tough task. I was only a young boy and needed sleep; Dad was not with us and Mum slept in another room. I was alone with Tru on our hard timber bed, and I had to handle him when the epileptic fits came. This helped me develop a habit of sleeping more lightly and being vigilant so I could help Tru when needed.

In summer, Dad's trips to the jungle or the provinces up north close to China seemed easier. But in winter it was difficult for him. Winter in North Vietnam can be bitterly cold, with strong, dry, chilly winds blowing from Tibet, the Himalayan Plateau, and northern Laos. Dad had to travel hundreds of kilometers north and west against the raging winds on an old pushbike. It was bitterly hard. He was not a macho, physical man but a small academic. He had neither shoes nor socks, only rubber sandals, and no hat. With few clothes available, he would wrap himself up with whatever material he could find to keep warm.

When I saw him slowly peddle off on his pushbike in the cold rain, searching for a cure for his son's illness, I knew how much he loved us. He had devoted his whole life and energy to his children. When I later became a believer in Christ, it was easy for me to call God my Father, as in my mind I remembered my earthly dad's efforts to humble himself and work hard in the hope of protecting and saving his children. How mighty is that picture of having the Creator God as my Father.

In 1973, after the Paris Peace Treaty was signed, there was a lot of joy in North Vietnam. People had something positive to look forward to because the war was finally over. But in the months after the Paris Peace Treaty, when the major battles were over, the consequences of the war engulfed us. A substantial number of young men from my village, including from my family circle, were now confirmed dead. During the war the government had covered up these losses. They could hide the reports then, but now there were no excuses. My second brother-in-law was confirmed dead. It was never easy for my sister and her two young children. Cousin Cuong was also confirmed dead. Another four distant cousins shared the same fate. With all these bad reports of death in the family, my parents drowned in shock and sadness. In their mid-50s, life seemed harsh and filled with heartache.

By this time my school work had become less of a priority to me. I felt so fragile. Nobody can focus on academic work while their emotions are overwhelmed. Another cousin, also named Cuong, gave me the bad news, when we were at the school opening: "You have to repeat Year 6. Mrs Suu has decided you can't go into Year 7." There were tears. I expected this result because many times Mrs Suu had warned me. I understood the consequences of failing. But I couldn't help it. I was punished for not being able to function academically. I had learnt a hard lesson.

That day I walked home from school with my head down, buried in shame. For a couple of days it seemed my head would never be lifted up. I decided to run away from home, and I did. But I could not run very far, or for long. For several days I hid among the trees in my uncle's thick garden. I lay there, ignoring all the calls, paying no attention to the frantic search by the whole family. Only hunger and thirst made me return home.

My sister Vien was also a teacher and married to an army officer who had died in the war. She had become a widow at a very young age and lived many miles away. When she heard about my failure in school, she came and advised my parents: "Uong should go to my school and live at my place. I will be responsible for his education; otherwise, he will remain uneducated and have no future."

I heard the conversation and quite liked the idea of leaving home to stay with her. During school days there was nobody around to play with anyway. I wanted to go back to study, but I did not want face Mrs Suu again. And seeing my classmates studying in a higher level was not a great comfort.

Dad, however, did not agree with Vien. "He must stay with us, and he will have to retrain. I do not think it is wise to let him go to your place because he is difficult and no one can handle him. Besides, he has to take care of Tru." Dad stopped and thought, and then gave more reasons for his disagreement. "Sending him to your school will not help. Running away only creates more emotional callousness. He must face the consequences. He must remain in this school."

The verdict was cast. I had to remain at home and repeat Year 6 in that school. I had no option. It was a total disappointment, but I could not change my father's decision. I knew he would not budge once he had made up his mind.

Repeating Year 6 was torment. I never felt at ease with Mrs Suu even though every day I had to call her *cô giáo,* the respectful Vietnamese term for a female teacher. Dad was a traditional teacher, so any sense of disrespect towards another teacher was unacceptable in his family and would be dealt with severely. I could be stubborn, I could fail academically, but I would not be allowed to fail morally in that way. "Respect the teacher and you will gain wisdom," I often heard him quote. So I was made to face and deal with my demons. I wish I had had good artistic skills to vent my feelings in those moments. Yet I finally overcame that hurdle. Being young and having a good family supporting me, I somehow dragged myself along and finished the year. But I could never feel close to Mrs Suu.

Despite all of my parent's efforts, Tru never got any better. Every time the epileptic seizures attacked, his body would shake violently. They always left behind the marks of injury. Each time it happened I could see the sadness, the frustration, the anger in my father's eyes. Many times I saw Dad cry silently in the dark, raising his hands in despair, asking whosoever for help to make Tru normal.

In those days, Dad's former teacher, Master Ngo Duy Can, the descendent of a Mandarin family renowned for its contributions to Vietnamese literature and politics, came to help. The Ngo family lived not far from us. Master Can was very old, but he came to visit my family quite a lot on his pushbike. Whenever he visited, two of my surviving uncles also came in to serve him because they had all trained under this great teacher.

The old teacher charged his pupils to be "more responsible for the honor of the family and the school of thought". The harsh reality of life under the Communists and the sickness of children were not good things. They could destroy "our good name and honor". Because my uncles had encouraged Dad to take strong drink to subdue the pain he had undergone over two decades, especially during the time when Tru became an invalid, the suffering seemed to have overtaken him. Master Can advised that Dad should "encourage Tru to get married and have children to bear his name" because they had all but lost hope of his recovering. This would need to be an arranged marriage. Mr Can's advice helped my parents see Tru's life from a different perspective.

In the meantime, my third sister, Vien, saw that I was home alone a lot with Tru. Therefore, each time she returned from Hanoi, she showered me with gifts as a reward for being a good boy. There were not just sweets but children's books from the

Kim Dong Publishing House. I had more chance to read widely and develop my curiosity about literature and poetry. Vien also liked foreign authors who had been translated into Vietnamese—Tolstoy, Mark Twain, Pushkin and Dickens, just to name a few. I also enjoyed them immensely. I have always been thankful for her special investment in my life. It helped me develop a reading habit and form my mind, and God used that mind to defuse the Khmer Rouge interrogation and torture that was to come in the future.

Tru was soon married, and now his wife, Thu, could take care of him instead of me. Sometimes I followed Dad into the forest and helped him harvest medicine. Through traveling with him I learned the art of survival in the jungle. I discovered which tree bark I could eat, which types of leaves were poisonous, and which fruit were edible. Much later, when I was lost in the thick Cambodian jungle, I knew how to survive and even apply medication to my own wounds. Then I realized the Lord had been preparing me in advance.

Tru died from an epileptic seizure during a meal one week before Tet (traditional Vietnamese New Year) in 1978. We were having a party and all waiting for the old year to pass and expecting the new year to come, with new hope. Tru was eating when the fit came. His whole body seized up so hard that the food spilled out of his mouth and nose. He probably died from choking. Tru passed away in my arms, and the pain of seeing him die was immense. He also left behind two young infants, instantly fatherless.

By that time I was a young man, hardened by injustice, anger, and the reality of war. I had learnt to bury my emotions, but the cry for vengeance sometimes engulfed me. At Tru's funeral I could not shed any tears, but I cried inside. Now the old questions I had asked myself so long ago, when Tai was killed by the American bomb, came back: *Where will Tru go? Will I ever meet him again? Is there an afterlife?*

Still the only reply was silence.

Chapter five

ANGRY ADOLESCENCE

As a young boy, after Tai's death all I wanted was to become a soldier. I dreamed of being a fighter pilot so that I might fly an airplane up into the skies above my country, search for my enemies and kill them to satisfy the urging of vengeance in my heart. When I heard planes zoom over my head, often I would raise my fist, running after them, shouting, cursing, throwing rocks at them, and promising to repay them for the blood of the innocent victims of war. But I was only shouting at thin air. The pilots, in their faster than sound machines, had already passed me when I made those threats.

Tru's sickness also triggered more drama within me. I became a moody young man. Often something inside me would boil up and explode. I had no idea how I had turned out this way. Most of my siblings were well behaved and presented a face of my family that was acceptable. They brought home praise and my parents were satisfied with them. I did not bring home praise and behaved in a totally opposite way. Physically I was also the darkest in the family, so with that and my attitude they gave me the nickname *Ba Ðen* (Black Boy).

I was angry with the world around me, with the country, with the people and with the poor state of my family. I could not enter ordinary high school because I was not up to standard. As well, many places in schools were saved for the children of soldiers who had sacrificed their lives in the war. I had no complaint about this; I just felt sorry for myself that I had not reached the brilliant level that could establish my own place in high school. As a result, I went on to study with adults in a *bổ túc văn hóa*, a special college, and therefore had more time to cause trouble in the village.

When youngsters are angry and have no formal outlet to express it or to voice their frustration, they can be dangerous creatures. Dad had practiced self-control; he had endured hardship. He had patience and remained virtuous. He had a duty to protect the family honor and the school of thought he had been trained to impart. But I had no thought for virtue. I didn't have to protect my family name and I had no tradition to represent. Marxists, or Maoists, were all about revolution and overthrowing the established order. I did not follow them, but I liked the idea of overthrowing everything. This deadly idea was injected into my numb soul. If Dad had not been perceptive and patient enough, I don't know what I would have turned out to be—a man or a beast with a sharp brain. All I wanted was that somebody should pay for the things they had caused.

The first focused target of my anger was the village representative. He was the first Communist Party member in the entire village. I was angry at him, his family and his relatives because all other families in the village had members who had died in the war, but his family did not. None of them had joined the army and none had gone to the frontier, so they had not been through the same pain as others.

"His family has not sacrificed and they have no real power," I told other boys. "He has no right to tell us what to do." The youth all agreed.

More and more I took matters into my own hands. My friends and I had neither position nor authority in the village, so we rebelled against the law. The only law to us was conscience, which I also thought I did not need. It was easier to roam the village than to listen to the voice of the heart. I soon formed a gang consisting of several young men whose fathers had died on the battlefield. We weren't always victorious; many times we were bashed up, and I would come home with black eyes or a bleeding nose. But I covered them well so Mum almost never knew. When a bad report came back to her, obviously she got angry, but at the same time she advocated strongly for me: "My son is innocent!" I knew I was not.

The poor Communist Party member often avoided confronting me or my family about what I did. He was strong and could beat me into submission, but the next day his children paid for it. He had to work while I had free time. He knew he was facing a demon and could not win in the long run. I had my gang, whose fathers were martyrs in the war, and the dead had become their guardians. We had more support and were better equipped than the Communist Party member. He had no voice because he had no moral ground to support his claim, and the villagers paid little attention to what he had to say. In short, he represented the village, but my gang was running it.

My family saw that I had become a young man full of anger and a mastermind behind the attacks on the Communist Party representative. They wanted the gang to stop its evil behavior. But I was stubborn as a donkey and angry as a rhino, and they often gave up telling me off. Besides, most things were done behind my father's back and there was no evidence of wrongdoing.

Young, and ignorant of my parent's sufferings, I became a stench in their nostrils. Every time Dad came home from a long trip there were heaps of bad reports. He was angry, but he could do little because I was now a young man, strong, mean-looking and arrogant. Also, I could reason with him as to why I was angry. He knew the injustice and unfairness in the village, as well as the blindness of the whole political system, but he was too polite, too well known, to act foolishly. I didn't have to follow his way.

In his frustration, Dad foresaw that if nothing was done to change my behavior, I would bring shame to his family. One day during noon siesta he could not sleep. I heard his voice calling in an unusual tone.

"Uong! Follow me. I have something to show you."

I followed him out of respect. He took me to the fish pond in the garden, and there my father the teacher gave me a visual lesson I could never forget.

"Do you see that large piece of concrete in the fish pond, son?" His finger was pointing to the object.

"Yes, of course I see it. What about it?"

Still pointing, he continued. "No one pushed it down there." His finger shifted to point to the thick bamboo beside the pond. "The bamboo shoots over there, day by day, week by week, month by month, year by year, pushed it in." With his teaching skill, he knew how to pause and let the idea sink in. "From the middle of the garden, that piece of concrete was pushed to the edge and then pushed down into the fish pond. Do you see it?"

Without waiting for my answer, he lowered his voice like any good father talking to his son. "Patience, son. Patience. The living tree, with patience, works the best. Anger and impatience are the tools of a fool, and never achieve anything that lasts or has real value."

I was very upset with him, but at the same time amazed at the visual lesson. I had thought previously that the large slab of concrete had been placed in the pool, though I had no idea why. It had no purpose. Only now, after my father showed me, could I see that it was the innocent, tender bamboo shoots that had pushed a big, heavy object from meters away. The lesson of subtle patience was clear, and the moral application to real life touched my mind a lot that day.

But did it change my attitude? No, it did not; it only changed my way of carrying out my attacks on my foes. I became more strategic and cunning in my thinking, but my goal was unchanged: to bring harm to my enemies, real or imagined.

Many years later, after I became a believer in Christ, I never felt at ease with my past activities. The Lord convicted me about restitution, which I carried out as honorably as I could. The first time I went back to visit my family, in early 1992, I approached all the families and people I had caused pain to, apologized for the evil things I had done to them, and genuinely asked for their forgiveness. The Vietnamese have a good attitude towards forgiveness and are willing for reconciliation. This brought healing and reconciliation with families.

Nowadays I am a child of God and know I am saved through Jesus Christ. Through faith in Him, and through the work of the Holy Spirit, I began to understand the source of my anger. Self-centered and self-righteous anger stems from being disconnected from God. This disconnection caused me real frustration and anger. But God has done a delicate work in my life, like a surgical operation, that has profoundly changed my soul. He understood my real issues. I gradually understood the power of forgiveness and let the Spirit of God lead me to practice self-control. From knowing who I am in Christ and what He has done for me on the cross, I can forgive. I know I am heading towards the future, and this great knowledge is truly a blessing for me. Knowledge about the nature of God and my life in Christ has helped me to ease my frustration at injustices and those cries for vengeance.

After the unification of Vietnam, many ordinary Vietnamese thought the war was over and that they could enjoy the long dream of peace. But that dream did not become reality. Tension on the border erupted in a dispute between Vietnam and Cambodia over the killing of many Vietnamese migrants in Cambodia; as well, the Pol Pot genocide was in full swing. As a result, as many as seven divisions of the Vietnamese army crossed the border to invade Cambodia in 1978, aiming to kick the Khmer Rouge regime out. This excursion angered China, Vietnam's giant neighbor and archenemy, and caused the Third Indo-China War in February 1979.

As a result, Vietnam again had to mobilize its masses and conscript hundreds of thousands of young men to join the army to defend its borders. I intended to join the army when I was 18. By law I had to, but my second brother, Tam, was already in the armed forces, so I was spared to allow me to stay home and take care of my parents. Only when Tam left the army in 1981 did the local government rightfully enlist my name for the army.

The day I was called to join the armed forces and leave for training camp was a day of joy and relief for the Communist Party member and his brothers. However, before I left home I went to the door of his house with a severe warning: "After I leave, if you and your brothers cause any pain to my parents, my siblings or my friends, then when I return from the war, you and your family will be finished!" The family of the Communist Party member took the warning seriously. Perhaps they were now older and wiser in their way of dealing with the village. Maybe they had learnt the hard lesson that, when they tried to hurt the villagers, who were their immediate community, they could lose their support; and obviously this was not a wise move.

Chapter six

TO CAMBODIA

In June 1983 we were informed that our whole regiment from the training base would be sent to the K front (code name for the battlefield in Cambodia). Before we left, we were rounded up to hear the base commander.

"Comrades!" he announced. "We have trained you. You have shown us your ability as soldiers of heroic Vietnam. You will now follow in our fathers' footsteps."

He quoted our ten pledges of allegiance to the army of Vietnam, which we had learnt by heart. These incorporated our moral standards as soldiers of the People's Army. At the end of the pledge we had to say, "Fulfill all duty, accomplish all tasks, and have the will to defeat all enemies."

The commander was quite young but already held the rank of major. He was quite a good motivational speaker.

"Our regiment will be going to Cambodia to carry out the task of *Nghĩa Vụ Quốc Tế*, international peace keepers. Tomorrow you can all go home to your families, but for two weeks only. You are to say goodbye to them." He then congratulated us.

It was a short announcement such as armies always give. We had heard him talking, but the only thing that was in our minds was that we were going home to our families, then to Cambodia. We did not know much about the war there, nor about our real task. However, we were excited about leaving the training camp. At least we would be free from rigid training programs. I had never been away from home for so many months before, and it would be the first time I had been back to see my ageing parents. It was an awesome feeling.

The two-week holiday with my family went fast. Families of soldiers departing for the frontline often threw farewell parties, and my family was no exception. All my family members came to say goodbye. They were convinced I would be away for only three years. "The war in Cambodia is nothing compared with all the other wars that previous generations fought," they said to each other. It was normal for them to make this comparison, but as a soldier I later found out it was no less dangerous than other conflicts. It seemed my relatives and the villagers all trusted the government. They were sure I would come back home in one piece within three years. It was total blind faith in official propaganda.

The next morning when I was leaving, almost every family member escorted me to the entrance of the village. Every departure involves a lot of emotion, and mine was deeply emotional for my mother and sisters, nieces and nephews. The men knew how to bury their emotions, but the women didn't. They were convinced I would come back, yet the thought of separation for three years was still too much for them to bear.

I was able to remain emotionless—the sign, I thought, of a courageous young man ready for war. But I tried to avoid looking directly into my mother's painful eyes. For the whole two weeks' holiday I had been unable to say goodbye to her properly. The last night at home with my family was especially hard. Summer was hot and everyone was talking, but everything I had to say to them was superficial. I was outwardly trying to look like a cocky, tough soldier, but inwardly I heaped up denial of my emotional reality.

"Three years away is a long time, Uong," my sister Vien said. "Dad and Mum may not be alive when you return!" Perhaps she saw my emotional void. Her words were a warning of my regret-filled future, but as a naïve young man I paid no attention. I heard what she said, but like everyone else I foolishly assumed I would come back. I reasoned that if I allowed myself to display emotion, it would not help me look good on my departure. In fact, I was running away from my heart.

As I departed from the village, I tried to find some courage. I looked at my mother and abruptly said, "Mum, everything will be all right! I will return in three years." It turned out to be a false promise because I had no control over the future or what happened to me. After saying goodbye to my mother, I turned away as fast as I could to avoid seeing her tears.

This departure was a painful regret in my mind for years to come, especially in the hard time when I was in a Khmer Rouge camp as a POW waiting to die. On the other hand, had I said goodbye nicely and allowed Mum to cry freely, or had I been less cocky and held her hand, and allowed myself to cry—or at least to identify with her and accept her pain—I might not have held on through my suffering to see her again. The time of departure for an unknown war is critical for the emotions; the acknowledgment would have helped to ease the pain for her, or at least freed us from regret. Thank God that He sustained and rescued me in those later troubled times, and when I finally returned to Vietnam after ten years, I allowed Mum to talk and cry openly.

(The day I returned, Mum, now much older, walked slowly towards me, reached out her hands, gasped "My son!" then collapsed on the roadside. I was just quick enough to catch her in my shaking arms. It was a deeply emotional reunion.)

The strange and notable thing about my departure from the village was that I followed the same route we had used years before when we escorted our many cousins who went to the south to fight for the unification of Vietnam. The only difference was I was not going to fight within my own Vietnamese borders. The cousins I had escorted before, in the late 1960s, never promised to return to their families. They were the generation of *Sinh bắc tử nam,* those "born in the North, but who died in the South". I was of the first generation of soldiers drafted for a supposed 'peaceful purpose'. The Communist government labeled us 'peace keepers', but whatever terminology they used, it was mere propaganda. I did not care much, and had no power to change it anyway. I only wanted to finish my duty as a citizen of my country. At the same time, I wanted to see other parts of Vietnam, my wounded nation, and fulfill the dreams of my childhood. I also wanted to see how terrible Cambodia was because I was extremely curious about that nation. I had read a lot about it and the perpetual killing of intellectuals and the middle class by the Pol Pot-Ieng Sary regime. Of course, all this information came from the one-sided propaganda of Communist Vietnam. Even though it was not all correct, I later saw the reality of this strange, war-torn country.

After everyone in my family had said goodbye, Ho, my brother-in-law, insisted, "Let me escort you a little further. I want to talk to you about my personal experience as a soldier in Cambodia." He had lived and fought there for several years. His regiment had taken refuge there and built the camps during the war against the Americans.

Of my surviving four brothers-in-law, three were soldiers; all had returned, but Ho was the most experienced as a man of war. He was a high ranking officer, but he was very down-to-earth and easy to talk to. He spoke to me that day not as a soldier or a commander, but as a brother. As we walked slowly along the road, he told me a lot about Cambodia, including some Cambodian words, though his knowledge of the language was superficial.

Then he said I needed to know more about the nature of the war there. "I am going to tell you something about Cambodia," he said slowly. "But you must promise to keep this information confidential because it concerns national security." His eyes looked intensely into mine. The look told me how serious he was. It was hard for him to share the facts because the information had the potential to leak, jeopardizing his position as a regional commander. But I was his brother-in-law. If he said no word, our relationship would be finished.

The promise was made and must remain within me for the rest of my life.

However, this much I can share of what he told me that day. "The war in Cambodia is now entering a very dangerous phase," he said softly. "Do you know that?"

I confirmed my understanding of the nature of the war as we had been informed during training.

Ho corrected my knowledge. "There are more casualties in Cambodia now than in the time the Vietnamese army invaded in 1978," he said. "In fact, I have some names of casualties and I am yet to inform the soldiers' families." Ho seemed sad when he told me this.

I was a bit shocked with this news. I knew Ho would not lie or deliberately try to scare me at this critical moment.

"The battle in Cambodia is now in a new phase," he emphasized. "It is about *truy quét* (search and destroy missions). The goal is to pacify the nation. It is from this that all the dangers come. You will fight against the Khmer Rouge insurgents, but remember you will also encounter international strategists, not the Cambodians alone."

What Ho wanted to say to me that day as we walked side-by-side was that I should be especially cautious since it was hard to identify friends and foes in the war. He knew I was a bit reckless. Or perhaps Dad had asked him to talk to me, for only a man of war like Ho, with his high ranking army position, could get me thinking.

As we talked I suddenly noticed Ho walking more slowly beside me. He was very quiet for a moment, and I followed suit. All I heard was the sound of our feet on the gravel. His steps were firm strides beside me—the steps of a living legend who had fought two famous wars, against the French and the Americans, and had survived.

"War is never easy," he broke the icy silence. "People like to talk about fighting, but it is never as easy as they think." He seemed very philosophical. "You will see how hard it is to face war!"

He paused for a long moment. Finally I heard a deep sigh, and felt his right hand on my shoulder, patting it. We were very much like school boys walking together.

"I will leave you to go on your journey," he said. "Be very careful and come back soon!"

I turned to look at him. His face had become that of an army officer, an experienced soldier, sterile and emotionless, not a brother-in-law or the friend of just moments ago. I saw his jaw close. We shook hands. It was a Western-influenced gesture.

He slowed to a halt and urged, "Go and be a true soldier, then come back to our parents safely!" Only a few steps away, I looked back at his face again. I mumbled something like, "Please take care of my parents for me." I knew he would.

I looked up then to the crowd of relatives in the short distance, to wave a final goodbye to them. They waved back to me.

"Goodbye, my beloved village." I turned, heading along the same route as many others who had gone before. My heart was racing. Now I was alone, yet my mind was occupied with the faces of every single family member. I wanted to look back again, but no; I could not. I should be strong. I should go out and take on the challenge of the world, and come back a different man.

Chapter seven

CAMBODIA IN THE EARLY 1980S

Ho's message did not sink into my mind until I arrived in Cambodia and then I began to see his point of view. Cambodia in the early 1980s was still a terrible place to be. Years of war had ravaged the nation and were the primary cause of its geographical scars.

Vietnam was bad, but Cambodia was even worse. On the train heading down to South Vietnam from the North, I could see the scars left by war on the Vietnamese landscape. There were thousands of bomb craters. Metal rails were strewn all along the rail line, especially from Thanh Hóa to Huế in the Northern Central area. However, nature had been kind to Vietnam's landscape. It had been about ten years since the last bomb had fallen in that area. Abundance of water from regular rainfall, mud, grass, and the work of farmers had covered most of the bomb craters, turning them into rice fields or fish ponds. I saw only part of the whole picture of Vietnam, but I could imagine the terrible war that had raged for decades. In Cambodia I didn't have to imagine anymore. The war there was still fresh and raw.

With such impressions etched in my mind, we crossed the Vietnam–Cambodia border without being noticed. Because the Cambodian and Vietnamese landscapes are no different, the only thing that showed us we had crossed into a foreign land was the patrolling soldiers, traveling with live ammunition around their bodies. Cambodia was still in a state of internal conflict, so soldiers had to be ready for combat.

"Do you know that we are now in Cambodia?" Kien, a young soldier sitting in the front seat of the military bus and peering through the windscreen, called back to the rest of us.

"How do you know?" someone in the back row challenged.

"You fool! Look through the window and you'll see. People here dress differently; they're in sarongs. The soldiers dress differently too, and they carry guns with live bullets."

We all looked through the window and saw that his observations were right.

I had read many books and articles about Cambodian life and culture, and now I was encountering the real land and people. I had sympathized with what they had gone through, and wanted to be a good and sensitive soldier who came with a helping hand, not merely a thug. But the words of journalists could never truly describe Cambodia or what I saw of the horror of war and genocide.

The first real Cambodians we encountered were along a river bank. Because most of the bridges in Cambodia had been wiped out, our transportation vehicles had to stop and wait for a ferry to take us to the other side of the river. I didn't know whether it was the Mekong River or one of its channels because we were not tourists and there were no tour guides to tell us.

Seeing us stop, many vendors came alongside the vehicles with local delicacies—all kinds of fruit, roasted creatures such as snakes, or insects such as crickets. Carried in baskets on their heads, the food all looked attractive to us because we were hungry. Some sellers could speak Vietnamese, others couldn't; but with food on display we knew what they were talking about. Money for food is a universal language. We had some money, but the vehicle windows were half closed and we weren't allowed to go out or buy local delicacies. Military Police stationed in that place made sure nobody left the vehicles.

During that long wait to cross the river, we peered through the window and noticed a house full of skulls not far away. One of the soldiers in our unit swore as he posed a question: "Why did they have to build such a large warehouse for those skeletons? What's it for?" He was not asking anyone in particular.

The soldier next to me showed off his knowledge. "I think the reason they built it and stored the bones right here is to make the living aware of the dead. They're the victims of this bloodthirsty regime."

Others also made suggestions. They talked to kill time. In any group of young soldiers, there will always be some reasoned answers, some mocking and cursing, and someone making fun of anything and everything. I leant on the window listening to all the talk, but I was tired by the constant travel and did not bother to join in. I wondered about Cambodia, its people, the war I had read about and, of course, the Cambodia my brother-in-law had told me about. My cigarette burnt red on my lips and between my fingers.

Of course there was a reason these warehouses had been erected—they were to promote awareness of the genocide perpetrated by the Khmer Rouge. For the three years of their Reign of Terror, from April 14, 1975 to 1978, they exterminated almost one-third of the Cambodian population of six million people. The warehouses of skeletons were the creation of political propagandists to promote the idea of a 'just' war and justify Vietnam's military actions.

Thanks to the atrocities of the overzealous Khmer Rouge, destruction was everywhere. After the Khmer Rouge regime was kicked out, the Cambodian soldiers and people went to the mass graves throughout the country and exhumed the bones. Skulls were put into piles, storehouse upon storehouse of them. The deep holes of the empty eye sockets stared at us naïve young soldiers. Everywhere we stopped for a break on our journey, we saw that the most prominent buildings were the large warehouses storing the skeletons, mostly skulls, of the Khmer Rouge's victims. Perhaps these were the only places where the buses could stop to rest, or perhaps it was a deliberate ploy of the propagandists to reinforce our sense of being on a just mission. Whatever the reason, the houses of bones were real, and totally confronting.

Pain and suffering were still etched on the faces of the ordinary people. At a glance, I could relate to what they had been through. Almost every surviving Cambodian had experienced the killing or disappearance of family members. Some had seen their whole family wiped out. It would take more than just time to heal those still alive. I doubted if many would ever experience a normal life again.

The warehouses of skeletons affected my thinking enormously. "Why did these things happen?" I asked myself. But the question was beyond my comprehension in those days, and the easiest escape was simply to blame the evil of the Khmer Rouge. Only later did I find out that any of us, given a chance by social pressure, or a nod from those in power, or the incentive of personal gain, or our own security, would commit crimes similar to those of the Khmer Rouge soldiers.

Later I realized it is not a matter of how Marxist doctrine, which advocated social justice, the equality of every person and freedom from class, turned out to be such an atrocity. It is ultimately the evil condition of the heart of man that causes this. Doctrines like those of the Marxists only help to unleash the evil of the heart. This was my discovery after I became a believer in Christ. I investigated and saw the effects on nations where Marxism had taken root. In Cambodia, Vietnam, China, Russia and many more, millions of people perished because of a dream society built on human thought. A numb soul, a seared conscience equipped with the deadly ideology of overthrowing everything, is indeed lethal to people. I am still glad about my involvement in the Cambodian war. At least the brutal regime has gone and can cause no more terror. I myself paid heavily for this involvement, however; it almost cost me my life.

Our regiment was eventually stationed northwest of Battambang, on the side of the Taren agricultural dam. Here I saw more of the nightmare of the Khmer Rouge. It was in this dam building, planned with the hope of providing water for all of the Battambang, Siem Reap and Pouthisat rice fields, that hundreds of thousands of Cambodians perished pointlessly. The Khmer Rouge never finished the dam, but the cost of poor management was the lives of countless innocent people. They died from hard work, sickness, malaria, and starvation as well as murder at the hands of violent, indifferent teenage soldiers.

One characteristic of the young Khmer Rouge troops was that they liked to throw the bodies of their victims into the waterways.

Skulls, therefore, could still be found in grasslands. Worse, before the soldiers ran away into the jungles, they systematically threw dead bodies into all the wells in an area so their enemies could not find water. As soldiers, we had to dig new wells because the previous ones were unusable.

The road from Phnom Penh to Battambang in the early 1980s was very much like a trail in a forest. There were few people. Monsoon rains, mines laid by the Khmer Rouge, and poor maintenance damaged the road even further. It seemed civilization had never reached this once busy route, one of the main arteries of Cambodia. We rode in Russian-built transport trucks with tanks escorting us. We were informed that there had been many ambushes on the way, so we had to be vigilant and hold fast to each other. For this reason, the army began to distribute live ammunition. It was a risky business providing young soldiers, straight out of training camp, in an unknown battlefield, with live ammunition, but we knew the Khmer Rouge would target newcomers like us to bring about a lasting psychological effect on us and nullify our fighting spirit. What else could be more effective than to ambush and attack new recruits in territory unfamiliar to them?

The army allowed us no prolonged rest on the way to the frontier. Firstly, this deterred many from attempting to escape, as not all soldiers wanted to fight. They only wanted to be peace keepers. Secondly, the military wanted to move as fast as they could beyond the danger zone, with its bad roads, young soldiers, and strange terrain, all of which were easy traps. If those young soldiers were attacked they would not know what to do and would only cause more chaos. And thirdly, the leaders of our training base sought to boost their image by successfully delivering their trained soldiers to the frontier without any trouble. They therefore encouraged the drivers to drive fast, to secure everybody's safety.

It was the journey of a lifetime for us young soldiers. Wherever we crossed a bridge that had been knocked down, I could see platoons of troops guarding us. They looked very vigilant, with live ammo draped around their bodies. The amazing thing was I hardly saw any Cambodian soldiers guarding us on the entire journey westward.

Chapter eight

THE RECONNAISSANCE BATTALION

The whole of our regiment was transferred safely to Battambang, a city in northwest Cambodia, around 4.00 pm exactly one week after we crossed the border from Vietnam's Tay Ninh province. We drove into what appeared to be a school yard, with everyone tired and confused. We were all looking for a place to rest when suddenly a loud whistle blew and a shout of command broke forth.

"All line up!"

The commanding word scattered the confusion. It was short but clear, without the clichéd 'comrades'. Within a minute, all of us ran into line.

A tall, skinny man in his early 30s, with a square-looking face that displayed the determined look of an experienced soldier, appeared. He did not wear rank or label on the collar of his green uniform, so nobody could identify who he was or what he was going to do. However, we all realized he had some sort of distinct authority. He strode slowly and firmly into our lines, along with two other soldiers much younger than himself. They looked into the face of every soldier and then handpicked 36 of us, including me. Those selected were ushered to form different lines.

"Why are we the only ones lined up over here?" one of the soldiers, whom I would later know as Boi, asked. (He eventually became a professional sniper and a good hunter.)

"Why ask?" I whispered, giving him a dirty look. "You're a fool. I'm just like you and don't have any idea. Besides," I snapped between my teeth, "we're not supposed to talk in line. You don't want to be a target for unnecessary punishment in this new territory, do you?" He fell silent.

The strange young soldier, meanwhile, left the lines and went into his temporary office. Within minutes, two army trucks reversed into the school yard.

"All of the selected ones in this line—up into the trucks!"

We all skillfully hopped into the vehicles with our gear. As the trucks were covered with canvas canopies, I only had a brief chance to wave goodbye to Chiêu, my cousin, San, my village friend, and those I had trained alongside in North Vietnam. From then on we were permanently parted.

All this happened in less than half an hour. The two trucks ran out onto the muddy road traveling fast, heading northwest towards the jungle. We were led by one M113, an American-built armored personnel carrier.

It was almost twilight when the trucks stopped at a camp surrounded by thatched huts. We knew we had reached our final destination. Later we learnt that it was Taren, a notorious place in northwest Battambang.

"This way—to that hall." A skinny, sick-looking soldier welcomed us and pointed to a large thatched hut occupied by soldiers. After we dropped our gear and put it in order on the dirt floor, we had a moment of perplexity not knowing what to do. The older soldiers were looking at us.

"You guys need something to eat and drink?" one of them asked. Later I knew him as Dung, but we nicknamed him *Map*, meaning 'fat' because he was bigger than any other soldier around.

Then other soldiers gathered around. They lit kerosene lamps so we could see each other properly. We were welcomed by many in this totally strange place. Drinks from fresh coconuts were thrown at us. We could indulge as much as we wanted to. A large bag of tobacco and some fine paper to roll cigarettes were also passed around. Soldiers from hard-fought battles were famous for two things: they smoked like chimneys and swore with every second word. They also seemed careless about everything.

"Why do you guys sit and eat like that?" one older soldier asked mockingly. "Leave the training camp and its stupidity behind!"

The other older soldiers laughed and demanded we relax. Some of us looked at them, wondering what they really meant. "You're on the battlefield now, not in the training camp," they encouraged us.

The older soldiers seemed truly more relaxed and careless about life than we new arrivals were. We were intense, scared, and tired. Yet the welcome and hospitality of those older soldiers gave us a sense of release and we caught the atmosphere of enjoyment. That night the tight order of the North Vietnamese training camp was abandoned, and we functioned differently from then on.

While we were eating, laughing, listening to the swearing, and talking about Vietnam with the older men, we suddenly saw everyone stand up and salute a figure who had entered the hall. We followed suit, recognizing the person as the strange, skinny officer. He gave us a big smile, saluted in return, and waved with a gesture for us to put our hands down.

"This is our big brother, Mr Kang," one of the soldiers announced. (Later I knew him as Sy, our platoon leader.) "He has something to share with you." He introduced Kang as our captain and second-in-command of the battalion.

Kang wasted no time in introducing himself; he welcomed us and basically told us that he was very proud to have us on board and that he would be our leader. He moved to shake our hands. I looked at him more closely. Kang had quite a handsome face, despite the harsh conditions of being a frontline soldier. When we were close to him we could see that he had a manner, a smiling face and a kind of personality that eased the atmosphere. But as captain of this special battalion, Kang was also a man of few words. As such, he successfully portrayed himself to be someone who preferred action to talk.

"It is dark now, so have a quick bath in the river or well nearby, eat some food and get a good sleep," he urged us. "But before you go to wash"—he turned to speak to the older soldiers around us—"You guys can choose the replacements you need." The older soldiers who had welcomed us were actually leaders of platoons and units. Some of their men were due to return to Vietnam and we were to take their place. They had already observed, through interacting with us, who they wanted. The selection was quick.

Before we dispersed to bathe, Kang told us, "Tomorrow morning, at 7:30 am, I will come to tell you where we are, who we are, and the nature of our task in the future." He then left for his thatched hut with his lieutenants.

After more than two weeks of constant moving on trains, buses and trucks, we had finally arrived at a place where we could rest. Having a good wash in the well nearby and some food and sleep was sweet for all of us. On this first night we also introduced ourselves to each other and became brothers in arms with the older soldiers, among them those we were to replace. Some had spent a number of years in Cambodia. They were happy because our arrival meant their desire to return home to their families had become a reality.

Kang kept his word and arrived at the hall at 7:30 am, army time. We were lined up, but he dismissed that strict, rigid style from training school and instead asked us to surround him in a semicircle. He then stood close to us and addressed us like an older brother who cared; he did not shout in our ears like the sergeant major in the training camp. Kang allowed us to take it easy, but his words were slow and firm.

"Do you know where you are now?" he joked to start with. "You are not in an ordinary army unit. You were selected to join this sapper unit, *Trinh Sát* (Reconnaissance Battalion) No. 27. It is directly connected to the Divisional Commander."

Kang paused and looked around the group.

"We in this battalion are the eyes and ears of this frontier. As a matter of fact, we are the most important battalion in the whole northwest of Cambodia. Our task is not fighting, but intelligence work. It is the most tedious, meticulous, and dangerous job in the army. The army's success or failure totally depends on us."

When I heard that I had been selected for this special unit, my mind was full of wonder and excitement. "I am in this dream team! Me! *Me!* We'll be doing dangerous things!" Most of the others seemed equally excited about our special soldier status.

"Secrecy is paramount in our work," Kang went on, "so there

are many things you will have to learn to conceal. You will be writing letters to your families, but you are not to mention the work." Only later did I learn that all our mail was routed through an address in Ho Chi Minh City to keep our exact location classified.

Kang peered at us once more; he looked happy because he himself had selected us out of the whole regiment from Vietnam.

"Now I have one last thing to mention, but it is very important. All the training you have undergone does not apply to this new task. You will have to retrain here in this camp." Pointing at the platoon of experienced soldiers who stood near us, Kang emphasized, "These excellent soldiers will be training alongside you."

Hearing about retraining, our hearts sank with apprehension. It seemed Kang understood how we felt. He smiled to ease our fears.

"The training here is not like that in the training camp. It is all practical. You can shoot live ammunition—without any charge— and it's fun! You will begin the training two days from now. Meanwhile, you have two days to rest."

Kang dismissed us. Some of the older soldiers took rookies to the garden where they planted vegetables; some went into the jungle to hunt and fish for food. We began to explore the place, not knowing the harsh reality of war was a very short distance away.

Everything in this training camp was different. The strategy of cross-pollination, matching us younger soldiers with older hands, gave us a taste of the reality of war and the art of survival on the battlefield and in the jungle. The battle-hardened soldiers used live ammunition and shot directly at their targets. We were often amazed at their skill in all aspects of fighting. When they had fun, they seemed to enjoy it the most, but when they were on task, they were very serious soldiers. They played hard but also worked hard in preparing for war. To this day I salute them.

The training was deliberately dangerous, with the intention of maximizing our fighting, observing and data-collecting skills in the jungle. We were learning new tactics in guerrilla warfare. Every day we went to the jungle for drills and shooting, and for practice in the art of neutralizing mines and re-using enemy ordinance. Dismantling live mines was potentially lethal, but that was the reality of training. A minor mistake would cost a life in an instant. All day, every day, we learnt how to cut through the jungle, use maps and compasses, and avoid making noises and silly mistakes. And absolutely always, no one was allowed to leave any trace behind them. If the trainers found some trace or mistake, they were not happy, and we had to redo the exercise again and again until they were satisfied. The art of survival in the jungle when there was no food or water, or when we were lost, was also addressed.

Most of us came from the Red River Delta region of North Vietnam, so to adapt to life in the jungle was never easy. Besides the hardships of training, the Cambodian jungle teemed with mysterious blood-sucking insects, ticks and leeches of all types. The most feared was the Anopheles mosquito. Many of us succumbed to malaria and could not function after only a few weeks in Cambodia.

After a few months of this intense training, I was once again selected for something special: to work in the communications unit within the battalion. Kang and the leadership were looking for the four sharpest, best-educated personnel in the new group to be trained by the battalion's communication experts. In this small, tightly knit, secret unit of eight, we became a family. No place in the world could have been more bonding than this fighting unit. We trained, worked, functioned in every way together. (Only later, in the reality of war, did I taste the bitterness of betrayal.) We were introduced to the communication equipment and, to my surprise, much of it was US-made. The PRC-25 field radio and other valuable American machines were our first choice. Our unit preferred this revamped radio because it was lighter, more compact, and much easier to transport than Russian- or Chinese-made equipment. It also consumed less energy.

Kang and the battalion leadership observed their new soldiers closely. They were very happy because what they expected from us materialized. We functioned so well, and progressed in all aspects of Cambodian warfare so quickly, that most of us went along with older soldiers on many short-term excursions into the jungle, commanded by experienced leaders, to test how we coped with the terrain. Within the first six months we were involved in tactical reconnaissance in the jungle. We helped sharpen map drawings, identified objects, detected Khmer Rouge activities, found their trails, and handed over all the information to strategists to plan attacks.

My biggest involvement was in the dry season campaign in 1983–1984. Military intelligence gave hints that the Khmer Rouge camps were built along the Thai border, so our task was to go into the jungle to take note of their activities and mark the exact location of their camps. We were to find where their firepower positions were and, if possible, determine the capacity of their resistance, so that later our infantry units could finish them off.

This campaign, however, was to be my last.

Chapter nine

THE CAMPAIGN

A s a soldier in Cambodia, one of the most challenging experiences of my life was that of guerrilla warfare. Most Khmer Rouge soldiers killed in action by the Vietnamese army were credited to the special units that went out into the jungle and lay in wait along the trails. They would ambush the Khmer Rouge with Claymore anti-personnel mines, which were American-made and modified by Vietnamese army engineers. Ambushes were a means of eliminating enemy combatants in minutes. Those ambushed often had no chance of survival. Normally, after the first round, soldiers came forward and finished their victims with a 'mercy bullet', then left the scene as quickly as they could.

But this kind of hit-and-run guerrilla warfare, perfected by Vietnamese soldiers in previous wars, was now being copied by others who knew the jungle terrain much better than we did. And as more and more inexperienced Vietnamese soldiers came along, jungle warfare became ever more treacherous.

In Cambodia, as usual every year during the dry season, the Vietnamese army fanned out from their stations into the jungle to weed out insurgents. We knew that in northwest Cambodia, near the Thai border, as many as 10,000 resistance groups were hiding. They used guerrilla tactics to engage their attackers. Their troops were small in number, but they were highly organized, experienced in jungle warfare, and determined to fight a war of attrition. They had strong support from many sources, and had proved throughout the years that they could bring lethal destruction to Vietnamese forces.

As Kang had mentioned to us before, the sapper's task was always the toughest in the army. No other job was more dangerous than reconnaissance in the jungle, especially when the enemy already knew our tactics. They could lie in wait on a high hill or near a water fountain to eliminate us. Khmer Rouge cadets had trained alongside the Vietnamese before 1975, when many regiments of the Vietnamese army were stationed in their land. Ho, my brother-law, was in one of these. Because reconnaissance meant intelligence gathering rather than fighting, we sappers were only lightly armed for self-defense, and always tried our best to avoid confrontation with any sort of enemy. Nonetheless, many times the hunter became the hunted.

Normally, the leader of a reconnaissance unit was an experienced soldier or someone who had been in the jungle for years, so he knew the terrain and how to spot or avoid danger. Experienced soldiers develop natural instincts in jungle warfare. Nevertheless, this time, the campaign assigned to us was under the command of Lieutenant Nguyen Anh. He had just finished training at the Army Academy in Son-Tay, west of Hanoi—one of the first young graduates trained specifically for the art of reconnaissance.

Three weeks before we went into the jungle to carry out our task, most of the experienced older soldiers complained and opposed the selection of Lieutenant Anh to lead us. Their objection was that he was far too young, too new to the terrain, and too inexperienced. Their protests were met with scorn by other leaders. "He has to start somewhere," they stated. As the decision was already made, there was no reversal.

The soldiers' objections also did not deter Anh; his determination to show them that he could be a trusted leader motivated him even more. He was from Ha Tinh Province and had a big ego, so he wanted to outdo all other officers. He was not shy in proving his critics wrong about his ability. Prior to our campaign, Anh personally selected and trained a group of soldiers who were willing to take a risk in his maiden operation. He did not know this campaign would be both his first and his last.

We had an unusual ritual in our branch of the army. Before

we entered the jungle for a major campaign, we always had a big party. Alcohol was allowed, but not too much. Near the end of the party, we all yelled, "Bottoms up!" and finished our drinks. Then everyone had to participate in the following ritual.

The leader would call, "Comrades! Those who are appointed to the campaign, stand up!"

We stood.

"Now, go to everyone in the unit and say a final goodbye! Also, apologize for any mistakes or offences, and ask for forgiveness."

We had no idea about the psychological effect of this approach, but in the army, especially in this unit, orders had to be met with obedience. To ask for forgiveness was a strange thing, but it was the word of command and we had to obey. To openly and squarely admit to and cancel one another's offences was a good principle, even if it did not come spontaneously from the heart. I do not know when this practice came into our battalion, but it was good preparation for those who would be wounded or killed in action. Somehow, the army hoped that by doing this we would be free from worry or guilt. We would also be free from the pain of future regret, or the pain of not having said goodbye, or of failing to be nice to comrades at the last moment.

Later on, when I decided to follow Christ, I discovered that the issue of forgiveness and canceling debt was not merely an idea, but a divine command. I had to live towards others with His forgiveness. But with God it is not something I am forced to do. I am inspired. God gives me joy as I forgive offences, and because it comes from the spontaneity of the heart, my joy is increased.

That night, half drunk, I took courage and approached each soldier, one by one, then smiled and apologized. I did it as a ritual, like everyone else. It was nonetheless an emotional goodbye for all of us because we were fully aware of the nature of the risk we faced. Some might be killed in action and never return. However, as soldiers we had to be prepared for anything.

That party, I later recognized, was a life-and-death party. And now, even more than 20 years on, I still appreciate it—the way we held each other's hands, looked into each other's eyes and asked for forgiveness. Although it was a ritual, I have no regrets about soldiers who perished in the war, or from malaria or other diseases. I will never see many of them again, but at least we said something nice to each other before we parted forever. I had no complaints about them and they had no complaints about me.

The Cambodian jungle was thick. As a reconnaissance tactic we were never allowed to walk on the same path, or to follow any path someone had walked before us. We were not allowed to take the easy way. If you found a path, you had to immediately cut across it and leave behind no trace or trail. Secrecy was our top priority, so we could not cut trees or branches or destroy foliage. We also could not afford to be wounded by mines or to be sick on the way. We had to be fit and to function to the best of our ability as a man in uniform, because if just one of us was wounded or sick during campaign, we were failures already.

Most individual soldiers knew how to read maps, clear mines, set directions by compass and cut through the jungle to reach a designated destination. We had to approach in one direction and go home by another. That principle could not be violated. My knowledge of this tactic was limited because I was trained to be a communicator, but I had the assurance of protection from our other troops. My priority was to keep the communication flow free and clear. The words of the two commanders, the one at the front and the one at home base, had to be perfectly matched. In those campaigns, communicators were the ears and eyes, heart and mind of the operation.

It took many days for us to reach the mountaintop codenamed '318'. "We've arrived," Lieutenant Anh whispered as his finger pointed to the spot on his tactical map. "Let's have some rest before we go further."

His intention was to establish our command center on this mountaintop before we sneaked into a nearby Khmer Rouge camp to collect data. "Our designated task is to infiltrate around this hill codenamed '416'." Anh indicated an area on his map dotted with red pencil marks. "It is just over there, less than a couple of hours walk." He looked satisfied.

To come this far from the base had been a tough task for us. Besides all our weaponry, ammunition, communication equipment and spare batteries, we also had to carry enough dried food and water for the whole campaign. Manpower was the only power source we had, and to cut through thick jungle and find new paths was really tough. Yet none of us showed any signs of sickness, and we had already accomplished 30 percent of the campaign task.

We sat down on the mountaintop, which was close to the Thai border. From it we could see, with the naked eye, houses and other big objects down on the northwest side of the border. Through binoculars, we could see cars and pickup trucks belonging to Thai soldiers and border patrol personnel.

"We are now in the heart of the Khmer Rouge-controlled area," someone whispered, and with signs we were warned, "Be more vigilant and cautious than before."

All the soldiers lay down on their backpacks and took some rest. Lieutenant Anh signaled for two men to be watchmen and go to their posts. Anh also called me closer to him and signaled that my activity as a communicator was to begin. He wanted to report to base and listen to the regional strategists.

I turned on the radio but got no signal. I turned it on and off a couple of times, but still nothing. Dung Map, my immediate communications leader, saw what was happening and whispered that we could not make contact from our position. "The distance between us and the base is too far," he reported to Anh. "This is also not a very high mountain. Our attempts to communicate will fail."

I could see the expression on Anh's face. It told us all about his indignation and disappointment, but we couldn't change the facts. The PRC-25 had significant advantages over other field radios, but it also had its own black spot. Its wavelength could not go very far in jungle and mountainous areas. Both Dung and I tried hard again, changing to a new set of batteries, but our attempts were futile. We could not communicate with the commander at the base.

Dung made a suggestion. "You must climb up that tree and face east," he whispered. His pointed finger directed my attention to a tall tree near us. "Place an antenna up there so we can maximize the wavelength." I followed his instructions.

Lieutenant Anh had already given me a short notice to relay:

We have arrived at the designated destination. All is well. Have found some suspect objects, evidence of heavy activity. We are ready to listen to your command. I looked at this short message, which I had already translated into code. All I had to do was relay it to the central commander, and then I could come down.

I was halfway up the tree to do my duty when the attack occurred.

Boom! Boom! The earth beneath me shook violently from B-40 grenade explosions. Blaring AK-47 assault rifles chattered over the deadly sounds of other machine guns, grenades torching and exploding, and the shouts of the Khmer Rouge charging: "Cho! Cho! Cho!" From the treetop I could see a number of dark green figures on the western side of the mountain shooting, shouting and racing towards our position. It happened so suddenly that the Khmer Rouge guerillas had almost instant control of the situation.

The thought flashed across my mind, *We're being ambushed!*

Lieutenant Anh was no doubt stunned by the sudden assault, yet as a well-trained soldier he also reacted well, courageously returning a few shots at the charging Khmer Rouge. His AK-47, however, was a lone voice in the chaos and had no impact. He ran for cover, commanding his soldiers to return fire: *"Hỏa lực! Hỏa lực! B-40! Bắn!* B-40! Return fire!" His shouting was met with silence—our soldiers were in a state of shock, and no doubt many had fallen victim to the enemy gunfire already.

From the tree I could see a few of our soldiers trying to reach cover among the rocks and behind trees. They were frozen for the moment and so was I. A few shots came from our position, but they had no effect on the charging enemy. No one could withstand an ambush at such a close range—our minds required at least a few seconds to realize what was going on and there was no time. Besides, the soldiers were already extremely tired from the journey. No doubt the Khmer Rouge had been waiting for us. What we thought was a safe position on the mountaintop had become a trap.

I began to realize that our worst case scenario, which we had tried to avoid at all costs, had now become a reality. Perched on a tree branch, I had to find a way down as fast as I could. Quick thinking was needed to get myself out in this situation, or the attacking soldiers would turn their guns on me. Dropping the antenna, I hid among the branches and looked for a way down. Waiting for the perfect moment, I literally dropped from the tree, almost jumping but grabbing a few branches with my hands to prevent a complete free fall. I don't know how I did it.

The noise of my movement attracted the hunters. Blaring gunshots were aimed at me. I felt the bullets zip scarily over my head and past my side. The tree trunk was my protection that day. The Khmer Rouge soldiers were so close, but by a miracle all bullets fired in my direction did not find their target. I thank God for that tree, which blocked all the bullets fired at me.

I landed on my back and rolled quickly away because I knew B-40 or B-41 grenades would be launched at that tree any second. As I scrambled away, two or three deafening noises exploded behind me, but all missed their target again. The mountain slope, trees and rocks prevented shrapnel coming in my direction.

However, I could not move very far beyond the next few trees. I waited, breathing quickly, alert and ready. Suddenly I felt the barrel of a gun poked into my side. I sensed the death call. I thought it was the Khmer Rouge. I turned slowly to see my captor and couldn't believe my eyes. It was Dung, my friend—my leader! He appeared so suddenly, as the Khmer Rouge had done. His actions were extremely unexpected. A quick glance and I saw his unusual, flaring eyes turning white and red. They were small yet looked very angry, almost furious. There has never been a scarier moment in my life.

"*Cấm chạy*! Do not run!" I heard his short, sharp command. I had no chance to sweat.

"Go back and retrieve the radio!" He gave the command through gritted teeth and was full of authority. I saw his finger on the trigger and remembered his shooting and hunting skills. He would not miss me. "Move!" He pointed with the barrel of his AK-47 in the direction of the radio, which I had left under the tree about 10 meters away.

I was now caught between two deadly enemies, and both were out to kill. The Khmer Rouge, on the one hand, knew the direction in which we were hiding, but not the exact tree. Dung, however, was less than one meter away, aiming his gun at me from point-blank range. At that moment, I decided, Dung was more dangerous than the Khmer Rouge. I looked at the distance across the slope between me and the tree where the radio lay. Calculating how many steps and how long I would have to run to retrieve it, I knew it was extremely treacherous and saw that I may not return alive. But there was no other choice. Dung would not change his mind, and the Khmer Rouge were waiting in the trees nearby to finish their task.

I tried to reason calmly. "Can you cover me and be a decoy to get their attention?"

"Just go and retrieve the machine!" Dung snapped without answering yes or no.

Obedience to a superior officer was a must; besides, his gun was aimed at me. I turned and jumped fast to hide behind the next tree, then a pile of rocks. I was about to make the next move when I saw the back of a Khmer Rouge soldier hiding behind another tree not far away. I aimed my gun at him, hoping to eliminate him before I ran to get the radio. I squeezed the trigger.

Paak! The bullet did not come out of the barrel of my gun. My AK-47 was now jammed, useless. Nothing seemed to be working my way. I lost all calmness, and another small mistake at that moment caught me out—a dry branch under my foot cracked, making more noise. All of a sudden, gunfire burst out and bullets whizzed around me. I have no idea whether Dung returned a single shot to distract my enemy.

Boom! The tree where I had taken cover shook violently, and the flare of orange-colored fire burst near me. The explosions knocked me out and threw me from my position and down the mountain.

When I regained consciousness, I was at the foot of the hill with no idea how I ended up there. The sky overhead was very dark; it seemed to be the middle of the night. I must have been in this place for quite a long time.

The first thing I did when I came to was to check myself all over to see whether I was hurt. Head . . . chest . . . abdomen all right. But when I moved my foot I felt a sharp pain, and I realized my toe was deeply cut.

"Oh, I'm wounded, but lightly," I told myself.

I had survived the ambush, and now I had to rest quietly and wait to see the sun rise. My comrades would come in search of me in the morning. Cold and fear engulfed me in the darkness; I worried that the Khmer Rouge would come looking for me. It was a sleepless night.

Chapter ten

LOST IN THE JUNGLE

"Wherever you find a rock, there you will find water."

Before that last trip into the jungle, we had often looked at the temple in Monconkherey, a small town northwest of Battambang. On the roadside there was a stone elephant with its head reaching out, as if it was running through the jungle. As young soldiers, ignorant of both Cambodian art and danger, we had pointed at it and laughed. "That elephant, the king of the jungle, had to run out of the jungle, while we are men who run into it!" It showed how reckless we were.

The northwest Cambodian jungle was the last frontier. It seemed as if no one had ever set foot in many places before. Wild beasts such as boars, poisonous snakes, tigers, bears and elephants still roamed the wilderness. The worst of it was that there were also human-made minefields, thousands upon thousands of them, laid out by both sides in the conflict, and the monsoons, mud, grass and fauna had covered them all. The enemy lay booby-traps and waited in ambushes. Danger lay in every single step, everywhere.

Now I was alone in this jungle. It was the first time I had ever been by myself in this fearfully quiet place. I lay where I had landed and did not know what to do. At that moment I still hoped someone would look for me, for we had been trained to recover our comrades if things turned out unexpectedly. However, it was a foolish expectation.

Even if there had been a mandate for the surviving soldiers

to return to the scene and recover the lost, this time it was an impossible task. A small unit like ours, out in the jungle so far from base, could do nothing to rescue its fallen. The Khmer Rouge had chosen their position perfectly. When they opened fire, many of their chosen targets were killed instantly. Had I not been climbing the tree, I too may have fallen in the first round. Now, without a radio or other communication personnel to ask for help, and without inside knowledge to pinpoint the exact location of the incident, it was impossible for me to send news back to base or for soldiers on other missions to know I needed help. The base commander would be paralyzed, unable to order the unit to regroup to look for a few missing members. The army did not have helicopters or other technology to carry out a rescue mission.

In fact, I had no way of knowing whether anyone in my unit besides me was still alive. Survival in an ambush was rare, maybe one in a thousand. It was only much later, in 1998, when I met some retired soldiers from our unit who now live in Ho Chi Minh City, that I learnt the truth. Four of our group of 12 never returned. Including myself, that meant five of the 12 were lost. The four weren't in the Khmer Rouge prison or the Thai refugee camp with me, and they never returned to their families in Vietnam. They were dead, whether wounded or captured and killed, no one knows; and still their families mourn their loss. Dung was heavily wounded and returned to base after a week to make a failure report.

Lieutenant Anh was discharged immediately after the aborted campaign. I haven't met him yet to ask how he feels after all these years. I still pray for him and ask the Lord for an opportunity to meet him and tell him what I saw from the tree, including his heroic act. It wasn't his failure; it was just an incident such as happens in any war. The knowledge might ease his pain.

After two days of waiting in vain at the foot of the hill and seeing no sign of any attempt to rescue me, I became restless and angry. *Nobody cares enough to come and rescue me,* I thought. *I can't wait to die here!* I decided to take action by making a move eastward by myself. It was a scary thing to travel in a thick jungle with no equipment, no guide, and a wounded toe. Yet my logic was that there would be thousands of soldiers in the jungle for the dry season campaign, so if I missed some, I would meet others.

I was preoccupied with the thought that I must return to report our failure and the result of the ambush. I was still on duty; my task was communicating with my superior, despite what had happened. The idea never entered my mind that I should cross the border into Thailand. Had I decided to cross the border that day, I could have reached it within a few hours, because I knew 'Mount 416' on the map was on the border. When we were on the mountaintop, one of our leaders jokingly said, "If anyone wants to go to Thailand, then that's the way." His finger was pointing at the buildings below us. "That's the big house of the commander of the Thai garrison stationed there."

We looked at him and smiled because no one in our unit had ever desired to go to Thailand. We were committed and proud of our army, our task.

My loyalty was part of my pride in the army's past achievements. The trust the army had placed in me could not be violated. Even in the current circumstances, I wanted to prove my worth. Going back to base, making a report and stating the facts of what truly happened to our superiors was crucial. I was willing to bear the consequences of the loss of the field radio. I knew all too well that, with the Vietnamese army, if you lost communication personnel or equipment it was equal to the whole battalion being wiped out. Yet I had to go back, despite the fear of shame and being dishonored.

But that was another big mistake. I totally overestimated my physical strength, and underestimated my wounded toe and the thickness of the jungle. Without a map and compass to guide me, I could not find the right direction. I was not equipped for this enormous task alone. Every day I could only move slowly for I knew I might be gunned down, whether by friend or foe, if I made a silly noise. The soldiers could not see and simply shot at the place where they heard something.

I struggled eastward for several days, following a dry streambed in the hope of finding water and my way out. It was another dreadful decision. I knew too little of the northwest Cambodian terrain. I tracked the dry stream until it ended in vast, tall grasslands, yet there was not a single pool of water along the way. The wound in my toe became worse, my shoes were worn out, and now the tall grass caused it even more discomfort. Looking across the grasslands, I estimated it would take me at least a day to cross them, and with no water under the scorching sun, I would probably collapse on the way.

Seeing the impossibility of my task I became desperate, frantic, and frustrated. Alone and wounded in the jungle, with nothing to survive on besides that stupid jammed gun, I totally lost my courage. The gun itself now became a heavy burden, and many times I wanted to throw it away to lighten my load. But I could not. "*Vũ khí bất ly thân.* Weapons shall never be separated from a soldier." Even if it was useless, I was convinced my jammed gun was the only evidence that would excuse me from condemnation.

As I went on, the jungle became more hostile and my thirst intensified. One thought kept ringing in my head: *You're lost. You don't know where you're going. You'll never make it back to base.*

Exhausted, I sat down on a rock not knowing whether to cry or grieve. I tried to force myself to be more reasonable, more collected. I searched my memory for data to determine the route back to base. My concern was still to change the tactics of my leaders—without my information, I feared that the whole season's campaign would end in disaster. More soldiers would be wounded or die. I felt the responsibility heaped heavily on me. I *had* to get back.

My strong will became my problem because I didn't know where to go. The dry stream had led to nothing. I couldn't even look up to the sun for direction, because in the thick jungle I could only see it when it was high in the sky, between 10.00 am and noon. I became terrified with the thought of dying in the jungle. Cambodia's mountain of skulls would grow by one more. No one would know it was me, a lost Vietnamese soldier, rather than a Cambodian victim, because I had no identification on me.

As I moved back down the dry streambed, I realized the hopelessness of my situation. I could not get back to base without aid. But where else could I go? The thought came: *Go to Thailand.*

No, it was not an option. To betray my army like the many deserters we had mocked before? No! Surrendering to the Thai authorities was beyond my thinking. Even though I knew the Thais remained neutral and would host me as a refugee, I was still a proud soldier in one of the world's most famous, disciplined armies. I had been selected and specially trained to serve in one of its finest battalions. I could not give myself up to them because I had never considered them worthy of accepting my surrender. I feared that my honor as a professional soldier and the honor of the family name I had inherited would all end with such a shameful act. How could I look into the eyes of my brothers-in-law? How would they look at me? I wanted to be respected, not despised.

But my dilemma only intensified. How was I going to get back to base? I didn't even know how many days I had been lost in the jungle.

The battle raged within me. Finally, I knew that I did not have a lot of time to think anymore. I had to make a decision. Live or die?

Seeing a mountain nearby, I decided to climb to the peak and look for the last time to see if I could get my bearings. After I dragged myself up, to my dismay, I could see nothing further. Here, on this unknown mountaintop, my heart cried hard, and I contemplated jumping off the cliff to end all the frustration and condemnation of failure.

I sat there, confused and saddened, considering my last options. Then, unbidden, into my mind came a vivid image of my mother. She was mourning and grieving. She cried hard, both hands covering her face, tears running down her cheeks, sobbing. She was waiting for my return! I had always loved Mum and had not said goodbye to her properly; and I remembered the hasty promise of return I had given to comfort her.

You don't have any right to end your life here, my heart urged, and that conviction ended my thoughts of suicide. I owed my life to my parents. The promise I had made to Mum was one I knew she had trusted fully. If I had to die at the hands of enemies, by wild animals, or by accident, that was fine, but to take my own life would be betraying my own words to her. I again weighed the choice of whether to live or die, but the image of my crying mother overshadowed all.

Looking back now, I have no doubt it was the Lord who

brought this image to my mind. Though I didn't know it, He was there with me in my perplexity and gave me the resolve to live. When depression and desperation seemed to overtake my life, he encouraged me to think critically and to choose to respect my life, my mother, and my promise to her.

Having made this decision, I began to go painfully down the hill and west towards Thailand. Every step I took brought with it a dragging sense of shame and guilt. The feeling was intensified by self-condemnation. *You have failed the moral standard of a professional soldier. You have let down the army's trust.*

Out in the jungle there was no one else—no friends, no enemies—only myself with the trees and the rocks and the smell of dead leaves on the ground. Yet that sense of guilt engulfed me. I had lost my honor as a decorated soldier and gained nothing. All I saw was a young man of failure. I tried to ease my misery by finding reasons to justify the disaster. *It was the leadership's fault,* I reasoned. *It was Anh's inexperienced tactics. It was Dung, who put me on the spot and then failed to act as a decoy.* But it didn't matter how much I tried to justify events; the campaign was a complete failure. And I, a proud soldier, was now heading westward to surrender, my future totally unknown.

This guilt and shame were only eradicated when I became a believer of Christ many years later. It was Christ who gave me rest (Matthew 11:28), Christ who set me free (John 8:32–34). Following the Bible's teaching, and the conviction of the Spirit of God, I understood how the Lord God had died on the cross for me. With trust in Him, I accepted He was able to take away all my shame, guilt, and failure. Instead of relying on my own moral standards, I learnt to rely on Him. My guilt and shame would have been lethal if I had not come to know the Person who had the authority and power to forgive and lift me out of my destructive way of thinking.

The decision to go westward had been made, but food and water were now the immediate need. I did not worry much about food because I could eat grass, the leaves of plants, and wild fruits to survive, but without water, living was impossible. I estimated I could go without water only one more day and then I would be finished. I had used up all my urine for water already; I had recycled it many times over and none was left. The wounded toe badly needed treatment and was the major factor in slowing my journey.

The thirst tore at my throat. All my mind and energy were now focused on thinking about water, but I could find none.

Suddenly an urge rose in my heart: *You fool, why don't you pray?*

Pray? I had never prayed before. But now, in this time of desperation, facing imminent death from thirst, I conceded that I was not an arrogant atheist anymore. How correct is the saying that there are no atheists in foxholes! There was no one in the jungle so I didn't have to be shy. I began to pray aloud without any hindrance.

First, I prayed to my dead ancestors, uncles, cousins, my brother Tru and my friend Tai. I made a lot of promises to them. I thought they had died young, so their spirits would be stronger and could guide me out of this miserable jungle. There was no answer from them.

Then, of course, I prayed to Buddha. I had never befriended him, but in my distress I didn't mind asking him for a favor. Once again, no answer was given.

Then I asked all the imagined gods, whatever names I could remember, to come and help. I asked them for direction and, above all, for water. The thirst had become so strong. None of the gods gave an answer.

And then I remembered something unexpected. "Why not pray to *Ông Trời* (the Heavenly God)? He is the highest and the best, so He could have the answer." Nobody had taught me about the Heavenly God; what I knew about the Supreme Being from Vietnamese culture was very, very vague. Yet we all relied on Him.

With this thought came a strange conviction: that this highest Being must be very holy, and if I did not confess all my nasty past and my sin, He would not answer my prayer. Terrified of approaching death, I began to confess hard, walking and chanting quietly in the jungle. Every deed, even my evil thoughts, came out of my foul mouth in prayer that day, with the hope that the

Supreme Being would hear and show me His mercy.

God did hear and answer my prayer that day. Out of the blue, a thought was planted in my mind: *Wherever you find a rock, there you will find water.*

Here in this mountainous jungle, rocks were plentiful, but water was rare. I began searching around the mountain's base. There were big rocks everywhere, and I went around them all. To my astonishment, after a few hours, a miracle happened. I found a large rock with a hole in it. It was as though someone had dug a hollow in its side, and in the hollow was six or seven liters of water.

I looked up, folded my hands, and for the first time ever seriously said the words "*Cảm ơn, Ông Trời.* Thank you, Heavenly Lord."

I looked into the water hole. The mosquitoes' larvae swam happily in it, which indicated it was drinkable. God immediately cast away my fear of being poisoned. However, I couldn't put my head in and drink to satisfy my thirst. The hole wasn't big enough. If it had been, I might have killed myself from over-drinking. I had to take a small leaf, make it into a funnel shape and withdraw a small amount of water so that I could sip. I sipped slowly, little by little, to ease my thirst and revive my dehydrated body.

I looked upward and again thanked the unknown Supreme Being. He had sustained my life. Then I lay down next to the rock and took some rest.

This waterhole became my treasure, but before long I had I consumed all the water. I then painfully decided to leave that comfortable place. As I walked away, the fearful question returned: would I find water again on the journey westward to Thailand?

Pained from my wounded toe, tired and extremely weak, I was determined to get out of the jungle before I collapsed. I feared malaria would strike me very soon because I had been in the open for days with no protection from a mosquito net, no medicine, no good rest or healthy food. Yes, the deadly malaria would come . . .

I had to get out of the jungle as soon as I could.

Chapter eleven

CAPTURED BY THE KHMER ROUGE

Còn nước, còn tát. (Where there is water, let's keep drawing.)

The Khmer Rouge were well known for their brutality and unpredictability. As soldiers we wanted to avoid being captured by them at all costs. The chances of survival for any of their prisoners were low. As I walked frantically westward, hoping to reach Thailand before malaria attacked, I did not know that I was walking directly into one of the Khmer Rouge camps.

The Khmer Rouge soldiers must have seen or heard me, hopping alone with torn clothing towards them. They lay in wait. Suddenly several figures sprang up.

"*Chob-shing!* Stand still!"

The loud Khmer shout from the bushes took me completely by surprise. I was shocked to hear yelling so close. With my first glance at these people I recognized that they were not Thai soldiers, not even Sihanouk's forces, but soldiers in black tunics.

"Khmer Rouge!" I gasped. My worst fears were now a reality. These were the genocidal, mindless, soulless barbarians I dreaded. There would be no welcome for me here.

I expected the enduring pain of torture followed by death. My mind worked through the fear, but my physical body was weakened by dehydration. I was exhausted, half dead and virtually non-functional. Not knowing what else to do, I stood there trembling in the middle of a dry brook, motionless, helplessly waiting for the worst to come.

Three of the soldiers separated from the group and slowly approached me. Another three remained behind, their fingers on their triggers, ready to shoot.

"*Dai daiy nau ca ba!* Put your hands on your head!" they shouted. The language we used to capture prisoners was now turned against me. I raised both hands above my head. Now I was like a fish in a net, not only being pulled out of the water but being placed on the chopping board, ready to be killed. It was a terrible feeling as I knew there was no escape.

One man reached behind my back and with a fast move grasped my jammed gun. Another reached for his red headscarf and used it to tie my hands behind my back and then tightly to my torso.

All six of them led me to their small camp. As we entered it, the sun was low on the horizon; it must have been around 5.00 pm The darkness of the night was coming. It was to mark the saddest day of my life.

I must thank God for that jammed gun and for my single-mindedness in carrying it with me, despite its being useless and a burden. It turned out to be a blessing. The Khmer Rouge checked it and found all the bullets were still in the magazine. It was immediately evident to them that I was a young and naïve soldier.

They gave me water to drink and a male nurse came to bandage my wounded toe. It was a total humiliation for me to be captured by the Khmer Rouge. Nightfall brought with it a dreadful atmosphere. I was now a prisoner of war, and I cannot describe the perplexity in my heart. This was an unconventional war, and the Khmer Rouge would not play by any rules. Everything about them was unpredictable. So prisoners had nobody to protect them. As my shocked state passed, I was aware of being surrounded by the world's most infamous killers.

My captors allowed me a short rest at this tiny outpost while, I presume, they contacted their commander about my fate. About an hour later a group of three came and took my arm.

"*Tau moh loukthum!* Go to see the commander!'

I was dragged to my feet. Even though it was night, my eyes were blindfolded and my hands were still bound, either for security reasons or out of mere mindlessness. My wounded toe played up painfully when I was forced to walk even as fast as a normal man. On top of this, I was exhausted and unbalanced.

We went on through the jungle for several hours. As the soldiers walked, one in front pulled me by a hammock rope attached to my body, and the two behind pushed me if they felt it necessary. Time and time again, protruding roots caused me to stumble and fall flat onto the ground. My captors giggled, but kept pushing.

"*Tau loun tik!* Go faster!" they demanded.

In those excruciating moments I silently cursed my decision not to jump off the cliff and end my life. But it was too late now.

Finally we arrived at a larger camp; it must have been close to midnight. I heard the noise of other soldiers exchanging small talk with each other. I didn't understand what they said, but I felt many hands grasp my body and limbs and lift me up. They placed me on top of a surface like a ping pong table. With my eyes still blindfolded, my four limbs were tied in an X shape to the four corners of the table.

Then I heard a command I understood: "*Deit!* Sleep!"

The Vietnamese uniform I was wearing was torn, shabby and in shreds, so my whole body was exposed to mosquitoes, which fed on me all night. I was terrified. It was very cold and my whole body shivered, but exhaustion brought me slumber.

The next morning, a group of soldiers arrived at the scene. They untied my limbs, removed the blindfold, and pulled me to my feet. For a moment the dazzling sunlight hurt my eyes. I could now see my captors face-to-face. They were both young and old, but all stared at me as if they could eat me alive. My body was stiff and aching from the position they had restrained me in on the table.

Someone in the line swore, moved forward, kicked my knee, and demanded, "*Kuiling!* Kneel down!'

Another young soldier brought a plate of rice and a few slices of radish and fermented fish and tossed it in front of me. Two or three men shouted, "*Hob tau!* Eat!" I had no heart to swallow the food while my captors stood watching me with murderous looks. They didn't care whether I ate or not, and soon two men dragged my half-dead body to a big tree away from their camp, surrounded by thick bamboo and wild vines. There they handcuffed my hands and shackled both my feet with a big chain to the tree trunk.

When everyone had left my presence and I was alone with my chains, I began to think hard.

This is it! I am now a prisoner. My life is gone. These people will interrogate and torture me to find out information and then kill me. My mind swam with pictures of the many thousands who had been tortured to death. I would endure the same fate, or worse, because I was a Vietnamese soldier. I trembled to the core. I was sure I would have to endure many deadly blows. Life in this cruel environment would not last long. How could I hope to survive?

In fearful moments it is easy for us to give up thinking and allow the situation to overcome us. I was fearful, but I still tried hard to think of a solution. I wanted to be ready for whatever happened. I was sure the Khmer Rouge would allow me to rest for two or three days, or even a week, while they waited for a higher-ranking decision as to my fate. But I could not be naively unprepared for something worse to happen. Nothing would be good for me in the near future, but as long as they allowed me to live, I had to be well prepared.

An idea came: *There have been many Vietnamese soldiers deserting to Thailand. I could tell the Khmer Rouge that I am one of those.* Weighing the pros and cons, I came to the conclusion that whatever I said, I must reveal something of who I was and at least some personal details. I could not just remain silent for I knew they were killers. I had already decided to live and go back to see my beloved parents, but would these people respect my life? No. I needed a strategy to elude them.

A Vietnamese proverb says, "*Còn nước, còn tát.* Where there is water, keep drawing it." When rice is germinating in a field, a Vietnamese farmer must save the seeds from drowning in too much water. If there is even a little water left in the field, the farmer will try his or her best to draw it out. I too was determined to try my best to save my life.

To what extent should I reveal myself? It was a tough question. I needed to keep crucial army information secret. I was a signal man, one who knew the communication codes, and those codes were worth my life. Even the commander of my unit was not allowed to know them. "The codes must be my highest priority. I have to protect them at all costs." But how could I conceal them from the enemy? I decided to pretend to cooperate with my torturers with the hope of outwitting them.

To think about pretending was easy, but there was another question I had to ask myself. How many soldiers in my unit had survived? And how many had been wounded and captured like me? I had no idea. If other soldiers had been captured, they would recognize me and I would be in even greater danger. "If I identify myself as a deserter seeking freedom in Thailand and a captured soldier identifies me as a member of his unit, I will have nothing to say." Another Vietnamese proverb says, "*Sểnh chân thì với được nhưng sểnh miệng thì không*". Words that are already said cannot be retracted", and I knew that these butchers would definitely kill me if they knew I had lied to them.

I was in total darkness, fighting this unimaginable battle alone. "Silence would not be a good strategy," I conceded. Seeing defiance from me would only fan the torturers' anger, so they would make me suffer more.

It was easier to think than to do. I was afraid my will was not up to the challenge. I knew the torturers would be coming very soon and would make my life hell on earth. They would use whatever was at hand to make me talk. They would inflict both physical and psychological pain.

They knew the terrain, so to lie to them I had to be master of my story. The Khmer Rouge had my body, but they could not have my mind. They were not dumb, just brutal, and their craving for information from their victims was greater than their feeling for a fellow human beings. Under torture I would have no time to think, so I had to set out a practical strategy now. I had to be calm and collected, and whatever I confessed had to be logical and consistent. I had to be able to control my conscious thinking.

Thank God I had read a book called *Bất Khuất* (*Never Surrender*) by Mr Thuan, an intellectual and a political wizard of the Communist revolution who had once been a prisoner of the South Vietnamese. I did not know why at the time, but before the campaign I had immersed myself in his writing. It must have been

God preparing the way in advance for me. I now had to practice what I had learnt from Mr Thuan. In his book, he told readers of his survival skills during imprisonment. All political ideas and agendas were now useless for me, but the art of survival in the hands of captors had become priceless.

According to Mr Thuan, torturers may screw your physical body to try to get information, but that information is still inside your head, and you have every right to say whatever you want to say. The hurt in the flesh is painful, but when you have made up your mind to say little, you must stick to that rule. The torturers do not know the information they are looking for, which is why they ask for it. If you are thinking logically enough, and are consistent enough, you can control them. You can be their master. It must have been the Spirit of the Lord that urged me to prepare in this way. I could not change my circumstances, but I could still be the owner of my mind.

The issue of Dung and his betrayal was hard—it bugged me and preoccupied my thinking. Now that I was handcuffed and chained to a tree like an animal, I resented and hated him even more. I wanted to think about how to carry out vengeance. But I had to tell my mind to refocus, to reprioritize, and not to allow itself to be distracted by unimportant issues. I could not afford to be obsessed about revenge on Dung. I had to remain calm and self-controlled. Every single minute counted in this deadly game.

My strategy was to visualize the torture in advance and what I must do to save my head. I had to train my mind in what to say and how to say it so that it was acceptable to the torturers. Not too much information, because the longer I talked, the more inconsistencies there would be. Yet I could not be silent; they would kill me if they felt I was not cooperating with them. My life was now entirely dependent on my collected mind.

This involved learning by heart everything I had to say. To help familiarize my mind with the information I would disclose, I invented a catchy phrase in poetic form so I could more easily learn, recollect and release the details. My worst fear was that under severe torture I would pass out and my mouth would say something I was not supposed to say, like a hypnotized person, and the torturer would use it as evidence of a lie. Then the consequences would be dire. I wanted my mind to be aware of this, even if I passed out. I had to be in total control.

Of course, I also had to utilize my deceptively youthful appearance. I didn't mind telling them that I was a special soldier—they knew that anyway from my uniform and AK-47. But I could also present myself as an innocent and naïve 18-year-old. The jammed gun was my evidence for this. The conclusion would be that this young soldier didn't know much, even how to use his own gun.

The Khmer Rouge were famous for their hatred of intellectuals. That is why they were willing to kill all of the able Cambodians. I therefore would not show them my knowledge. I would appear to be a simple, stupid young man, only knowing simple matters. The army codes would stay deep within me.

Three days later a group of five soldiers arrived at about 11.00am. In their hands I saw hand phones and other equipment, and I sensed the interrogation would begin soon. I was ready.

The Khmer Rouge were notorious for their use of simple objects to kill their victims. I had heard they even used palm leaves to kill. They choked their victims with urine or hung them upside down until they died. My captors, these interrogators, were those people.

When the group of five came to me, they had the fierce look of killers. No one said a word until the leader, whom I later knew as Oum Uot, spoke through an interpreter.

"You are in our hands," he began, and then made a simple demand: "*Hãy khôn ngoan cộng tác.* Be smart and cooperate with us. If you do not cooperate," he added, pointing to the three men standing around me, "they will kill you."

Even though I had had several days to prepare and rehearse, the presence of the interrogators made me feel a deep chill. I began trembling with fear.

The superficial questions, such as what my name was and where I came from, were soon over. I changed my name from Dang Uong to Van Uong—"Van" is a more common name in Vietnam and I wanted my captors to think of me as an ordinary, unexceptional person. I also explained to them the Vietnamese law of military mobilization and the fact that I had been drafted into the army, and as a citizen had to comply. The questioner started to accuse us of invasion. He lectured me on the failed morality of the Vietnamese government and army. He was confident the Khmer Rouge would triumph in the end. When he asked me how I saw the invasion of Cambodia, I answered by parroting that we were *Nghĩa vụ Quốc Tế* (International Peace Keepers) and said we had no personal plan to take Cambodia. I had no idea how bitterly the Khmer Rouge hated this term. I saw a smirk come over Oum Uot's face as the interpreter translated.

The three soldiers standing by did not miss the chance to begin their work. The first round of bashing was unleashed and they poured their anger into my body as if it were a punching bag. They were so brutal I lost consciousness.

The torturers did not go softly after that. No 'carrot and stick strategy' for them. The three went to work to maximize my physical pain.

One unlocked my ankle chains and made them even tighter, and then shackled my hands behind me with handcuffs. Following the initial shock of sharp pain, I could hear the 'click' each time I moved as metal blades squeezed my wrists tighter. Next my feet were pulled apart by two strong soldiers, one on each side. They yanked the chain hard to increase the spread. It takes professional dancers or martial artists years of practice to maximize the spread of their legs—practice I had never done. I heard a crack in my groin and a searing pain shot between my legs. When my feet could not be spread further, they bound them to a long bamboo trunk with each ankle resting on a joint of the branch. The whole of my body now leaned forward, half bowed down, half sitting up, in a falling forward position.

The interrogation proper began after that. For every question that I answered, "I don't know," I received a punch, a karate kick, or a bash with a club. I do not know how many times I was knocked out. The position of my body helped amplify the pain when they hit me. Every blow caused damage. Even if they had not beaten my body, they could have simply kept me in that position and I would have died in agony.

On the first day of interrogation, the torture finished quite late in the afternoon. The torturers untied my legs, loosened the handcuffs and, before leaving, gave a chilling warning through the interpreter: "We will come back tomorrow!"

That night, I could neither lie down nor stand up. I didn't know what to do with my body. Passing water was agonizing, and my whole body was in excruciating pain.

I had to undergo many days of different styles of torture at the hands of this group of men. The torture of the 'next day' was always more unbearable than that of the previous one because the bruises in my flesh increased the torment. Only when I passed out was the pain eased. One day, when my feet were again spread-eagled along the bamboo stick, they placed a plastic shopping bag over my head. Then a man named Boong Chian gave me a hard kick to the abdomen; I thought the whole of my intestinal contents were about to spill out of my stomach. I saw my vomit splash out mixed with fresh blood while I gasped for air in the plastic bag. There was quickly no oxygen left so I passed out.

I must have been unconscious for so long that the torturers thought I was dead. They threw my body into a hole to bury me. Thank God that when they began to cover me with soil, I awoke and cried out for help. My whole body was wet; they must have thrown cold water over me to try to revive me so they could continue my punishment.

The beatings had two purposes. One was for vengeance, because it was the Vietnamese army that had kicked the Khmer Rouge out of power. The other was to gain every piece of intelligence they could about Vietnamese strategies and movements. The vengeance was easier to bear because it was only paid out until the torturers were satisfied emotionally. The torture for information required more systematic, intelligent questions, and it seemed never ending. Of course, the Khmer Rouge strategists also studied the information I gave and checked it on their maps, because no one wanted to be outsmarted.

The worst form of torture was being buried alive Mongolian-style. As a young kid I had read about the cruelty of the Mongolian soldiers and the way they tortured and killed their enemies, but in the hands of the Khmer Rouge the stories became my reality. They dug a hole, tied my hands behind me and put my body into the pit. Then they completely covered it with dry soil up to my neck. It was hard to breathe because the soil kept following the contractions of my chest and filling in more and more tightly until I could only breathe a little. My thirsty body ached, but the worst part was thinking about how slow and appalling dying in this way would be. Flies nipped me around my lips, eyes, and nostrils, the vulnerable, sensitive places where there was moisture. Ants also bit me all over my face, ears and nose. I felt the bites, but I was helpless to defend myself. Terrified when I saw more ants coming towards me, my skin dripped sweat so that my body odor attracted even more insects and mosquitoes. They innocently made my suffering even more harrowing.

As a young man in my early 20s, bound arm and leg, I was tortured not just for a day, not just for a week, but on and on. Each time the Vietnamese army attacked or destroyed a Khmer Rouge camp, my body became a target for retaliation. The Khmer Rouge treated me not as a man and not even as an animal. To them I became a thing. They would beat me at any time, whenever they wanted and in whatever style they chose. The treatment meted out to me was so harsh that I was covered in bruises and cuts.

The abusive language was constant, beginning every morning. "We are going to kill you today," was their chant, mixed with deadly, murderous laughter.

One of the most feared torturers was a young boy of around 12 or 13 years named Dhara. He was truly a beast. I will never forget his face. He often ventured to my area about nine in the morning and kicked, punched, or bashed me just for fun. But with Dhara it seemed that torture by physical torment was not enough. Using a club or aiming his pistol at me, he demanded I undress; he then looked at my totally naked body, laughing at the bruises. That laughter was total humiliation. For many days, often using a bamboo branch full of thorns, he beat me, shouting.

What was on his mind? No one ever knew, but the way he exercised his pride and power over me was beyond comprehension. Dhara enjoyed seeing his victims' suffering. My Khmer was very limited, but I knew the language of cursing. *"Vey ngob alau ey. Ahn vay khalang, ahn vey ngob.* I will bash you to death. I will hit you harder. You will die at my hands." Every time, before he left the scene, he would raise his finger like a pistol and say, *"Cham moui ngai tiet bank ngob.* One more day and I'll shoot you."

For the first few days I took his threats seriously and waited to die. To tell the truth, a bullet in the head would have truly been a mercy. But as the days went by, I came to ignore his words and treat them as a joke, however deadly they sounded. Sometimes I heard someone shouting, *"Dhara! Ban hoi!* Dhara! Enough!" to stop him from carrying on. It must have been his leader, or his father.

I have forgiven him now, along with all the Khmer Rouge soldiers who made my life hell, because I myself have experienced the forgiveness of Christ. But such forgiveness did not come automatically. It took time to learn to exercise this valuable, eternal gift and commandment.

My hair still stands up and my skin gets goosebumps when I share about these experiences. My hands and my ankles still have the marks of those terrible days even though they happened more than 20 years ago. But my ordeal gave me something unexpected. When I became a believer in Christ and began to understand His agony on the cross, I was able to deeply appreciate His pain for me and the heavy price He paid for His world. In my case I didn't have to protect the army communication codes, but for the sake of my many countrymen, those who had fathers and mothers like I did, I chose to do it. The Lord God also faced the same issue. He chose the cross, the nails, the agony so that I and billions of people in His world could be protected by Him. Oh, how much I appreciate the cross of Christ!

Chapter twelve

MONSOON PRISONER

The dry season ended so the Vietnamese army's aggressive campaign to destroy the Khmer Rouge camps also ended. For me, as a prisoner of war under the Khmer Rouge, bound to a big tree in the middle of the jungle, the fearful physical torture reached its peak, and then ended when my captors saw I had nothing else to offer. Despite all they had done to me, I had never revealed the army communication codes I had hidden deep inside.

But another nightmare began. It was the monsoon season and the rains arrived. Whenever it rained, with lightning and thunder and fierce winds, I was totally exposed to the harsh weather with nothing to protect me.

The place where I was held had no roof or shelter, and the first time the rain came down I was soaked with water. I will never forget that night under a tree in the soaking rain and strong wind. Water poured down as if from buckets. At that moment I wanted to curse the day of my birth.

Water was everywhere that night. I tried to move around the big tree to take cover from the wind, which lashed me with the cold rain. At first this was successful. But when the water rose, the jungle insects began running everywhere to find higher ground. I was left alone trying to fend them off as they crawled up my body. I did not have anywhere to move because both feet were shackled in chains and one hand was handcuffed, and the space I could move around in was less than two meters square. The big tree was a good place for me to hide from the wind, but it was a good place for the insects as well. I am a man not a pig, yet I wallowed in the mud to prevent insects crawling up my body.

The morning after this first night of heavy rain, two Khmer Rouge soldiers came out to check on their prisoner. They saw I was in the middle of the mud, all wet and covered with dirt from head to toe. I looked so terrible they laughed and labeled me *chruc* (pig), then spat at me. The men brought some food on a plastic plate and placed it where the mud was, but they totally ignored my situation, despite my attempts to plead with them in sign language for a piece of plastic to cover me from the rain and a shovel to dig a hole to bury my waste.

"*Ot mien te! O cheut ngob hoi.*" I understood them to be saying, "We don't have anything to put on top of you as a cover, nor a shovel to dig a hole. You're about to die anyway, so why do you need to cover yourself?"

They left; however, later one did come back with a plastic sheet, a few pieces of timber and bamboo rods, and kindly covered the place where I was. But there was no shovel.

When the monsoon rains came, I no longer had to be vigilant against Dhara or the other Khmer Rouge. Their torture was now less deadly than the swarms of insects. Ticks, mosquitoes and leeches all searched for blood in my already worn-out body. Scorpions and centipedes, hunting for food at night, had no mercy. However, the worst by far were the hundreds of thousands of hungry, angry red ants. Whenever it rained, the water lay everywhere in that flat area, so the hard timber my captors had made up for my bed became dry ground and the red ants took refuge there. They were irritating, annoying creatures. They went out looking for food early in the morning and worked hard until late at night. They could attack their victim all day and all night long, persisting without ceasing. No wonder they can kill elephants! I needed sleep badly to recuperate from the torture and sickness, but the ants, ever hungry and working hard for their queen, deprived me of rest. I could not sleep, and that caused more irritation. Nonetheless, I dared not report it to the Khmer Rouge soldiers for fear that it might give them fresh ideas to make my life even worse.

With the rainy season came an explosion of mosquitoes.

I knew that if my situation didn't change, I wouldn't last long. Even if I survived the torture, the weather, the sickness and the red ants, I was guaranteed to die a terrible, slow death from malaria. Cambodia is one of the worst places for this disease in mainland southeast Asia. In my army unit, even with a doctor and nurses available, and giving us top priority in medical care, many soldiers could not function because of it. Most absenteeism was caused by malaria. Some even died. In fact, malaria was the main concern for the Vietnamese army and it crippled its capacity in Cambodia more than anything else. It was more deadly than ambushes, mines or conventional warfare.

With no mosquito net to cover me, no medicine to prevent infection, a wounded body, and internal bleeding caused by torture and the dreadful living conditions, I could not foresee any hope of survival. I lived and counted the days and waited for death to come. I would have preferred that the soldiers just take me out in the open, give me one or two shots in the back of the head and end my life with honor, rather than live the way I was then.

As I had feared, malaria came to visit me. It flared up only a few days after the first rains had fallen. It came so suddenly. I felt my whole body shaking violently like in an epileptic attack. I did not want the Khmer Rouge to see this so I tried to control it, but I failed utterly. When the extreme temperature raging within me met with the cold from outside, it caused my body to vibrate to generate more heat. Then this great heat surged through me and my head seemed to burst with headaches. I could not eat for days, and drinking water was rare because I was only allowed a liter per day. In my childhood, my mother said, "If Uong can't eat then I must run to find a doctor," because I never skipped a meal. But now, in this hell on earth, I had no desire for food. Every 48 hours I was attacked by malaria again and again. My body quickly wasted away.

The food I left uneaten became even more dangerous because it attracted insects. At first I ignored it, and then it became a horrible annoyance when I was badly sick. I didn't mind the flies so much, but when red ants found the food, they would call in their whole army, hundreds of thousands of them. They were everywhere.

My health spiraled downwards. I became so sick I could not even raise my head. My muscle tissue wore away. It was difficult even to lie on my back on the hard timber because there was no fat tissue or muscle left, just skin covering skeleton. Both sides of my body began to ache because of my protruding hip and joint bones touching the unyielding wood. It was even hard to turn over.

Although I could not eat, I would not prevent the Khmer Rouge soldiers from bringing food for me. They kept providing rice and fermented salted fish, their famous *bo-hoc*. When you are sick with malaria, the last thing you want to eat is salted fish. Leftover food, rank fermented fish, excreta and trapped water that formed a pool nearby were all major concerns. I had many times asked for a mosquito net and finally a guard named Barht gave me a broken one. At least now I felt protected from the mosquitoes and red ants, but the request for a shovel to bury the leftovers was again and again ignored. Now I could see the intention of the Khmer Rouge—they wanted me to die a gradual, painful death.

I was bedridden—I do not know for how long. Perhaps many weeks passed when I did not even have the energy to get myself to stand. I wished I could get on my feet and walk around the tree, but I was too weak and dizzy and I fell down like a little child learning to walk. It was a simple desire to be able to stand, feel the wind, and see the sunlight. But sickness made it an impossible wish.

I had had a big family who would care for each other when one member became sick. In the army there were nurses to look after us when we were ill. But now I was alone in the jungle with mindless people and soulless creatures. I felt utterly lonely and emotionally afflicted. Tears ran dry on my bed. I lay there thinking about my wasting body and those terrible red ants wandering around all day, all night. I was sure that when I became so sick and paralyzed that I could not move, the ants would come and finish my body off.

The idea of suicide again surged up within me. It became very strong. Once a person loses hope and sees no prospect of living, contemplating the end of life is one of the few ways to occupy the mind. I was sure the Khmer Rouge would not consider my life of any worth. What did I have to offer them? Nothing! They had murdered millions of their own kind because they did not see any worth in them. Had I had a gun and a bullet, or some other instrument that could end my suffering, I would have used it.

As the idea of suicide engulfed my thinking, I totally lost interest in living. However, God had His own way of communicating with me at those critical times.

One day, when I was very, very weak, I began to think about a bowl of soup, a spoon of sugar, a piece of candy, or even a lemon or star fruit. They became my fantasy. When someone is starving and sick in prison, food is a big preoccupation in their mind. I was no exception.

Suddenly a large frog jumped near me and started eating insects. I thought I would kill it, skin it and maybe ask for a fire to cook a nice meal that day. I lay waiting for the frog to come closer and closer. Finally I picked up a stick, aimed, and threw. The blow landed right on the frog, but either because the stick was not big or heavy enough, or because I was unable to throw it hard or was in a bad position, I only wounded the frog's rear.

The frog was shocked by the sudden blow. It croaked, jumped and rolled frantically. Even though it was severely injured and could hardly move, it was determined to crawl away from me. I tried very hard to reach it and kill it. Had I had a longer arm or a longer stick, I would have achieved my goal. It was only about 20 centimeters out of reach. For several hours I tried to catch it, but the chain on my foot prevented me getting close enough. Very slowly, the frog crawled away using its front legs, blood dripping from its rear. It rested when tired, yet it kept moving ever so slowly away. I watched it with frustration. I couldn't even have it for a meal!

Then a thought came to my mind: *If that silly frog, even though it is heavily wounded, is determined to live for another day, I too can live—live to tell my terrible story to the world. Who knows, one day I may.*

Thank God that He taught me a lesson that day. He opened my eyes to see His world. I realized that all the ants and other insects I wanted to kill were also determined to live. Even the tree leaves and bamboo shoots were trying their best to reach out to the sun, to breathe and live. I looked at the frog again. Before I had tried to kill it; now it inspired me tremendously!

Only a few days later the frog had recovered and was happily jumping here and there, but never again close to me. It made a nest just a few meters away where we could see each other. Whenever it was about to rain, the frog made the noise 'op op'. During and after rain it kept chorusing 'op op'. It also croaked to find its mate. I had all the time in the world to observe it, and that frog became my friend.

God used the creatures of nature to send me a message. I asked myself, "Why are these creatures, which are far lower in creation than me, determined to live? And why am I, a higher form of creation, attempting to end my life in the midst of this misery? Do I have the courage to live like that frog or those insects? Can I keep going for just one more day?" I cherished those humble thoughts, and the Lord God gave me a determination to live again. That decision was another triumph: "Live and live well despite the unbearable hardship." That was the urge, the unheard voice, that grew up in my heart.

At the same time, I was reminded of a dream I had when I was ten years old. I was falling into a scary, black pit. I was in hopeless free fall, plummeting deeper and deeper into the darkness. Suddenly a net with four corners appeared under me and prevented me from falling any further. The net then slowly drew me up from the pit of darkness. There, on the edge of the pit, I could see a great light. The light was so wonderful, so beautiful, yet very, very mild. Then I woke up.

At that young age I had no idea what the dream meant, and I had never disclosed it to anybody. But now in my prison, hapless and hopeless, I remembered it. There was no guarantee, yet somehow I had a strong conviction from the vivid image of that dream that I would survive. I took comfort from it. Somebody would come to rescue me, though I didn't know who. In the back of my mind God had injected an assurance, and even though I had not yet met God personally, I had that invaluable confidence.

My mind often goes over and over that time I was lost, lived, and overcame in Khmer Rouge captivity. I cannot forget to thank God who sustained my life and thereby saved me so I can tell others about my Benefactor. He saw that I had lost the determination to live and was very lonely. In his infinite wisdom He sent a creature and allowed my brutal attempt to make it food, knowing that I couldn't do anything to it and that it would strengthen my desire to live again. God imparted a little of His knowledge to me in that time of trouble and I found some joy. I am reminded of the greater Benefactor and Intelligence that stands over me as a human. Oh Lord God, you saved me in my most humiliating time.

The frog was my companion for a long time. Amazingly, it continued living near me. At times it seemed to look at me in defiance, but mixed with comfort. "You tried to kill me, you brutally wounded me, but I am still alive. I live to tell of your cruelty, but just look at me so you also can live."

The frog only ran away when the Khmer Rouge soldiers destroyed its nest at the end of the rainy season.

Chapter thirteen

A BASKET MAN

I had been trained to think positively, first under Dad, then in the army. Communist army commissars are experts at injecting positive thinking into their soldiers so that they can face the worst scenarios. But it was the Lord who put His words, His idea and His dream into me in my Khmer Rouge jungle prison.

I was sick and had nothing to do besides attempting to revive my strength. Sometimes I would compose poems in my head or solve math problems in the dirt with my finger or a stick to kill time. Captivity is a very boring life. One day I became aware of a group of young Cambodian women; they must have been the wives or relatives of the Khmer Rouge soldiers. They passed my spot every day going to and from their work sowing and harvesting crops and vegetables. But they had no bamboo baskets. They carried everything in their sarongs or *kama* (head scarfs).

There was plenty of bamboo around their camp and that gave me an idea.

Many times I felt the urge within me to 'do something'. At first I ignored it altogether because I didn't want to help these brutal people or create more trouble for myself. Besides, I was still feverish and sick from malaria; I couldn't even sit up properly let alone do anything. But the urge increased. It was a persistent nagging within me for many weeks. Eventually I couldn't bear it anymore, and I said to myself, "If I see anybody carrying a knife and bamboo in the next few days, I'll talk to them."

To my total surprise, the next day I saw a group of young

soldiers carrying knives and bamboo pass by. I took courage and called to them using a Khmer term of respect: "Boong!" They heard my voice, stood still, and saw me waving at them. After a moment of hesitation, two of them came closer. One of the men, who had a big knife, gave me a very strange look. I spoke to him in sign language—I still did not want them to know I could speak their language and understand their conversations. The sign language indicated that if he gave me the bamboo on his shoulder and a knife, I would make baskets for them. He looked even more puzzled, so I took a few grass blades and made a basket symbol for him.

"*Oh! Choong thur kah!* He wants to do some work!" he said to the others. He confidently handed me his knife and bamboo.

I had learnt basket-making from my father, who tried to teach me such practical things to counter my restlessness as a teenager. He himself had learnt the skill from other farmers. I asked the soldier to split the bamboo the way my father had taught me. I used all my strength to sit up, took the bamboo, made threads and began making a basket.

Two days later the first small basket was finished. I felt I had achieved something. The person I gave that first basket to, as a gift, became so excited. It was the first time ever during my imprisonment that someone had said to me the words "*Oh-kun ch'rona.* Thank you very much." Before long I was making many baskets.

I am sure it was the Lord who gave me the urge to work and convicted me about winning the hearts of my enemies. Now I had something to do to kill time, boredom and frustration, and it revived my desire to live. I also didn't mind teaching people how to make the beautiful baskets, and a few learnt, but many were too proud to be taught by a prisoner. They all liked the baskets I made, however, and I was glad to be useful. A prisoner had become their instructor.

News about a basket man spread through their camp and other camps. Many arrived to have a look and place orders. I knew I would have more chance of survival if more people knew I was there and was useful. That whole dry season I was busy making baskets of all sorts—big, small and even stylish.

Some kinds of baskets I didn't know how to make, but in that case I asked them to give me an old one so I could dismantle it and follow the pattern. In doing this, I helped the women and nurses in the camp carry out their duties. Of course, all the baskets were made free of charge. But from this activity I gained attention and received better rationed food. The nurses, who became fond of me, smuggled me some medicine, including quinine to help cure malaria (enough to take some and keep some spare for times of need). One day a nurse came and looked around to see if anybody was watching. Then she tossed me a toothbrush and mimed a tooth-brushing action. I nodded and thanked her. I had not brushed my teeth for many months and perhaps had bad breath. But I had no place to hide it, so the next day when a young soldier came and saw it still brand new, he asked in Cambodian about it and I had no answer. So the toothbrush was confiscated. I gave it to him cheerfully—my life was more important than a toothbrush.

Through making baskets, I acquired more tobacco. Like other North Vietnamese famers, I liked to smoke using a bamboo pipe. This functioned much like a Middle Eastern hookah, passing the smoke through water to trap the nicotine. The Khmer Rouge, who were all heavy smokers, chopped down a bamboo tube for me and gave me tobacco and a lighter. By miming the universal two-fingered smoking gesture, people realized I wanted *thnam chuoh* (tobacco). Everyone gave me a little, and in the end I had a bagful.

Smoking was a great benefit to me. When I made the baskets, I took the bamboo flakes which I produced when I polished the threads, and soaked them in the juice from my bamboo pipe. I then placed them all around my living area. It was an organic poison that prevented leeches, rats, snakes, ants and other insects venturing across my perimeter. It had a strong, bad odor, but I preferred to live in a stinking smell than to be exhausted from fighting the insects all day and night. I learnt this trick by accident in the days when my father was making medicine. We were cleaning his pipe one time and accidentally dropped the liquid on a nest of termites and ants. Suddenly we noticed them running frantically away from the nest. We tested it on more nests and discovered that insects didn't like the smell.

And it wasn't just insects it spared me from. Often when soldiers came close they swore, "Oh, the stinking *Juon* (Vietnamese)," and left me alone. Whatever they called me, they had no idea I was purposely chasing them away.

For the first time, the Khmer Rouge also now provided me with a shovel so I could dig a hole to bury my waste. The lack of hygiene invited insects to come and brought more sickness and disease, but prior to the time I made baskets, all my begging for a shovel was met with ignorance. I had used up the plastic on my rooftop, time after time cutting out a handkerchief-sized piece and placing my excrement and other waste in it, then tying it up with grass and throwing it with all my strength as far as I could into the jungle.

The Khmer Rouge intended to see me die slowly, but God intended to see me come out as a victor. I believe it was someone who received the free baskets from me, perhaps the nurses, who eventually informed the International Red Cross about me. And it was they who later came and took me away from that terrible outdoor dungeon of the infamous Khmer Rouge.

Chapter fourteen

MINH, THANH AND DUNG

I was well into building a good relationship with my captors
through basket making when one day around noon some soldiers
brought another a prisoner, a young man in civilian clothes, to stay
with me.

He introduced himself as Minh. He had escaped from Vietnam
in search of freedom and a better life through Thailand. He was
thin, big-eyed and innocent-looking. For me, in the death camp of
the Khmer Rouge, to see a person of my own race and nationality,
who spoke my language and shared my culture, was a treasure. I
was longing for intelligent conversation and an affectionate look. I
thought I had met an angel.

Unfortunately, Minh turned out to be very naïve and a total
disappointment.

The guards went off to lunch which allowed us to talk. We
started to introduce ourselves by giving our place of birth. Because
I had hidden my true identity from the Khmer Rouge, I decided I
could not tell Minh the truth. I said my province was Thanh Hoa,
as I had told my captors.

Minh looked at me. "You're not from Thanh Hoa!" he said.
"You must be from Hanoi, or somewhere in Ha Tay, because your
accent is not from Thanh Hoa."

I was shocked. Fear leapt up within me and made me almost
shut down. I began to shake, and I'm sure my face must have gone
very pale. Had the Khmer Rouge been present, they would have
noticed my alarm.

"Quickly!" I told Minh. "I'm having a malaria attack." I asked him to massage my neck so I could turn away from him and end the conversation.

I had lied to the Khmer Rouge—their interpreter had no idea about regional languages or accents in Vietnam. But I had never thought of that. Now I was in an extremely vulnerable position. Had the interpreter recognized my accent, I would have been dead. How on earth did Minh know? I had no idea. I feared that if he had a loose tongue, I would be in big trouble. I would be tortured again and death was a certainty.

Using all my courage, I fought to calm myself and control my shaking knees and trembling chest. Minh only thought he had to rub my neck because of malaria. Despite my best efforts, however, my insecurity intensified. The prospect of undergoing another round of torture terrified me to the core.

An even greater problem was that Minh could speak some Cambodian. I heard him chatting and laughing with the soldiers. He even pointed to me and told them, "*Anih contob*. He is a soldier," then pointed to himself and declared, "*Khnoum cheeh chuone*. I am a civilian." Minh thought I did not know Cambodian and never realized I was pretending to be simple to avoid the Khmer Rouge's infamous hatred for the educated. I knew Minh was naively playing with deadly killers, but I could not stop him. There was no point in arguing with him about my accent or my birthplace because arguing only magnified the problem. The Khmer Rouge would find out about our argument and then kill us both.

After that first noon conversation I couldn't speak much to Minh. All my thoughts were about eliminating him to cover up my deceptions. I feared he would detect more lies and report them to the Khmer Rouge. It would not be hard to kill him—I had plenty of things on hand that I could use to finish him off quickly and without pain. Since we were imprisoned in the same spot, and he slept a lot, it would be easy. I prepared a sharpened and smoothed bamboo stick which I could drive through his ear or nose while he was asleep; no blood would come out. If Minh ever told the Khmer Rouge where I really came from, I decided, I would act.

But once again the Spirit of God intervened, this time to prevent my evil action. The Lord showed me that to kill Minh was easy, but to dispose of his body wasn't. We were both chained to that big tree. Whatever I did to Minh would leave a mark behind, and the Khmer Rouge would not tolerate inmates killing each other. They would realize I was trying to cover something up, that I had killed Minh to silence any confession. Had the Lord not stopped me, I would forever be a murderer.

Three days later, the five Khmer Rouge soldiers who had tortured me reappeared. Seeing them again made the hairs on the back of my neck stand up. I thought, *They've come for me again!* But it was Minh they were after. They unchained him, ordered him to stand up and searched him thoroughly. First he was all smiles and very cooperative. But his mood changed rapidly when they searched his sleeve. They found a gold chain hidden there, sewn into his shirt under his armpit.

"*Ey te?* What's this?" a soldier named Boong Chian demanded, holding the chain in his hand.

Minh mumbled. He had lied to them before, saying he had nothing on his body. His face had turned completely white as though there was no blood left in the vessels. He knew he was in trouble for attempting to outsmart the Khmer Rouge. Trembling, he tried to explain in faltering Cambodian and literally knelt before them begging for mercy and understanding. Terror made him stutter and stammer.

Sadly, Minh's please fell on deaf ears. The soldiers bashed him terribly, striking him with karate kicks, gun butts and clubs. He was kneed up and elbowed down to maximize his pain. To prevent him from screaming out, they stuffed his mouth and bound his face with his own shirt. For a few moments Minh's face was fully covered with blood, and then he collapsed to the ground unconscious.

Being tortured had been hard for me, but being forced to witness the torture of another person, just a few meters away, was even harder. During my own torture I was often knocked out and felt little, but here I saw Minh's body being kicked and beaten, falling about in all directions. I saw him vomiting up fresh blood. He became a punching bag for five mad, heartless men. I wished I had the authority to tell them to stop, but I too was in chains, and they still could torture me any time they wished.

That afternoon, when they grew tired of bashing Minh, they chained him back up with a chilly warning, "*Chahm muoi ngai tiet*. One more day," and a throat-slitting gesture. It signified *ahn vey ngop*—death by beating.

Minh was restless and shaking that evening. "They are going to kill me!" he gasped through cut lips and a probable broken jaw. All my animosity and indifference towards him was replaced by sympathy. Nevertheless, I was speechless because we could do nothing to divert the Khmer Rouge's intentions. There were no words to sooth his worry and dread. Finally I said, "I hope their threat is just like the threats they gave me for months. I'm still here!" Minh seemed a little easier at the thought.

But that evening, when dinner came, they gave Minh an abnormal meal: extra rice, more chili and more fish than my portion. Now we knew they were not playing games; they meant to kill him by morning. He could not eat or sleep that night, and neither could I. We both lay looking up at the sky and no words came. Had I known the Lord, I would have offered a prayer during those terrible hours for his soul.

The only explanation Minh had for me was that his wife had been so concerned about his escape that she had carefully sewn the gold chain along the line of his sleeve under the armpit. Then when he reached a refugee camp in Thailand, he would have money to buy food and an envelope and stamp to send a letter to her saying he had arrived safely. He was sure it was hidden safely, not realizing the Khmer Rouge knew all the tricks.

The next morning I saw Boong Chian and another two soldiers take shovels to the western side of the camp. There they dug a hole behind thick trees, near a termite's nest. A couple of hours later, at about 10.00 am, they came, unchained Minh and declared, "*A Minh! Tau Bangkok*. Minh, you go to Bangkok." They talked further but I couldn't follow the Khmer; only Minh might have understood. They led him out in that direction without a blindfold. A short time later, two gunshots rang out.

After about an hour they all came back, shovels in hand,

and smiled at me. "*A Minh tau Bangkok hoi!* Minh has gone to Bangkok!" Then they pointed at me: "*Choong tau ey? Do you want to go too?*" I nodded a silent yes, pretending to know nothing. If they wanted to execute me that way, I was willing to accept it.

Later, after I was released, I still hoped against hope that Minh might somehow have survived. I found no trace of him during my five years in a Phanat Nikhom refugee camp in Thailand. When I later learnt English and was working for the Thai Red Cross, I checked with all the Vietnamese in Dong Rek refugee camp as well, but none knew of anyone by the name of Minh who had come to Dong Rek at about that time. I sent many letters through the International Red Cross looking for him as a missing person, but I never received any report back. My desire was to apologize to him for my evil thoughts, but I concluded he had definitely been executed that day.

After Minh was gone, I felt deeply guilty for my hatred towards him. He wasn't a bad person sent to spy on me; he was just a simple man trying to find his way to Thailand, and like me he had been unfortunate enough to fall into the hands of the Khmer Rouge. He lost his life in a horrific way.

I often ask myself: what if the Khmer Rouge had not found the gold chain in Minh's sleeve? Would I still have carried out my evil plan and driven a bamboo blade through his ear or nose to secure my own situation? I don't know. The more I think about it now, the more I understand how evil are the hearts of all men, not just the Khmer Rouge. All of us, when it comes to our own safety and when we are under intense threat, would willingly lie to eliminate another for our own sake. The more I know my heart, the more I appreciate the sacrifice of Christ for me. Only He could do such a thing as sacrifice his own well-being for others, even His enemies.

Perhaps, if they had given him more time, Minh would naively have shared his discovery about my personal identity with the Khmer Rouge, and I may have ended up being a murderer. It would have haunted me for the rest of my life.

Near the end of that hot season, the Khmer Rouge brought me another inmate. His name was Thanh. According to Thanh he came from Hanoi and was a captain in the 7704 regiment (a military police regiment based in Siem Riep and Battambang). For some reason, he had decided to leave his post as a captain in search of freedom in Thailand. He never had enough time to tell me why he did this. Like Minh, he ended his search for a better life in the hands of the Khmer Rouge.

Remembering how my time with Minh was cut short, I wanted to know more about Thanh and, if possible, assist him. I felt sure that, being a captain, he must have read more about the nature of the Khmer Rouge and would surely know what to do and how talk to them.

"Have they interrogated you yet?" I asked. Not waiting for an answer, I added, "What have you said to them?"

To my surprise he answered, "I've told them all I know about the Vietnamese army in Battambang."

I immediately realized Thanh was in great danger. It was probably too late for him already. To confess all he knew in one go was a grave mistake. The more you told, the more they asked, and talkativeness exposed you to being illogical and inconsistent. Thanh seemed never to have read about the dangers of torture; he was sure the Khmer Rouge would release him and let him go to Thailand as he desired.

I was deeply concerned for my fellow inmate because the five torturers had not yet come to him. He had developed no strategy to ease his pain in the near future. *The five monsters will come and make you suffer,* I thought. I had to inform him of this so he could quickly develop a defense mechanism.

Thanh, however, paid no attention to what I said. He thought that by telling them all he knew, they would not torture him. He was an officer with the rank of captain and should have known better, but somehow, naively, he told the Khmer Rouge his rank and everything about his work. He even spoke in Cambodian to demonstrate his ability to communicate with his captors.

"I'll be all right," he reassured me. "I've talked to a very high ranking officer. I'm okay."

"I hope so," I said to comfort him.

As evening approached I thought the Khmer Rouge would allow Thanh to sleep in my space. For me this was like having gold heaped into my pocket. I had not seen a 'normal' person for some time, especially one from North Vietnam. Thanh told me he came from Hanoi and his mother and sister were still alive. But I did not want to tell him anything about my own origins. I had a new identity and stuck with it whoever I met.

I looked at Thanh again intensely that evening and repeated my warning. "The Khmer Rouge will torture you for more information."

"I have told them everything," he replied. "I have nothing else to say."

"You'd better have a good rest. Think deeply and prepare a strategy for tomorrow. They will come and torture you to check whether your confession is valid."

The tone of Thanh's voice told me he was growing annoyed with my insistence. In my mind I had an uneasy feeling about why he was so trusting, even with the Khmer Rouge, but it seemed I could do little about it. "Hopefully they will trust you," I commented, and said no more. However, 30 minutes later he asked, "If anything happens to me, can you please tell my mother and sister?" I naively agreed to this and have since struggled because he gave me no clear address for his family. I was never able to contact them to tell them what happened.

Seeing the bamboo and half-made baskets nearby, along with the bamboo flakes lying around me with the strong smell of tobacco juice, Thanh realized I was making baskets for the Khmer Rouge. He even rebuked me for being dirty. "You don't have to work for these butchers," he lectured, urging me to stop. To this I only smiled and kept my secrets buried. He had no idea of the art of survival in this death camp.

As night fell, the Khmer Rouge leader ordered that we be separated. They took Thanh away and chained him to a tree 15 or 20 meters away.

Three days later I saw Boong Chian, Oum Uot and a few others, all in their famous black cladding, approaching. They carried a radio, a few plastic bags, knives and other torture equipment. There were more than six people in the group now, including Dhara. They approached Thanh's spot. My fears for him had come true.

For a short time after the group arrived, I heard the interpreter shouting, "If you do not declare more, these soldiers will bash you to death." Then the screaming of someone under great pain began. It was unbearable. With Minh the torturers covered his mouth and forbade his screaming or moaning. But with Thanh they did not. Now that Dhara was on the team, Thanh must have undergone dreadful cruelty. The noise, the shouting, the begging and the groaning made my skin crawl. Hearing the screaming of another human being in desperation has a devastating psychological effect. I closed my eyes and plugged my ears.

Thanh's greatest mistake was that he had revealed his rank of captain, his knowledge of the army and his years of serving in Cambodia. This made his interrogators believe he must know more than he had told them. The torture continued for several days. One night, hearing my coughing from another malaria attack, he shouted, "I'm going to die here, Uong. They have broken both my legs. I cannot move. Ah, the pain . . . " Even from where I was, I could see they had not broken his legs below the knee, but right up near the hip and groin. With his legs chained and two strong men pulling to maximize the spread, no doubt Dhara would have jumped on Thanh's body in this most vulnerable position.

Thanh soon succumbed to malaria and screamed a lot at night during the attacks. He yelled for medicine, asking guards to clean up his mess. He was ignored. I could hear his voice becoming weaker every night. I wanted to say something to comfort him more, or do something on his behalf, but I didn't have the language or ability to do so.

A little less than two weeks later, Boong Chian and two other men I didn't know came to me, unleashed my chains, and commanded, "*Tau! Moh a Thanh!* Come to see Thanh!" I cannot write most of what I saw there. Thanh had died of torture, but it was more than torture that had killed him. Over half his body was gone because of the ants devouring his flesh. His eye sockets were empty and his face was no longer the face of a man. The scene was horrible to witness.

Thanh had heaped up his leftover food and his waste. He had no strength to throw it away. With the torture, the broken legs, the malaria and the insect attacks, Thanh had lost bodily control. All his excrement had come out and he had been unable to clean himself up; it attracted even more insects. He died a horrifying and slow death.

The two Khmer Rouge soldiers threw a large empty rice bag at me. They said something I did not understand, but I knew they wanted me to put Thanh's body into that bag. When I touched it, the red ants turned to attack the thing that was disturbing them. I had no choice but to do the job as quickly as I could, or I would be dead like Thanh. The soldiers then buried him near the western side of the camp.

I had seen many people die in many ways, but Thanh's death was the worst. I could not eat for days afterwards. His deformed face being eaten by ants was hard to forget.

Why did the Khmer Rouge take me to see Thanh's body? I still cannot answer that question. Perhaps they wanted me to die an awful psychological death, or to let me know that my life would end in the same fashion. The Lord's hand was on me, however. If not for His special protection, I am sure somebody would have also had to carry me out with only half a body to bury and the other half offered to the ants.

As the next dry season came, I heard a very big gun battle somewhere not far away. It was about 3.00 am I could not tell its exact location, but the Vietnamese army must have changed its strategy because rather than artillery explosions I heard the explosions of rocket-propelled grenades. Later on I learnt the Khmer Rouge had used almost all its skilled soldiers to attack a Vietnamese commando battalion at Ta-cuong, in Battambang. This battalion had been sent to Cambodia from one of the best tactical divisions of the Vietnamese army, the 308 Iron Fist Division (as they called themselves). The Khmer Rouge attackers quickly overpowered the lightly equipped commandos and drove the battalion from its position. They also captured a young soldier named Dung.

Two days after the attack, the Khmer Rouge brought Dung to me to show him off as their trophy (this was a different Dung from the man who betrayed me). Unlike with Minh and Thanh previously, I had only a very short time with him. I knew they were going to torture him and I would have to listen to the screams of a young man again. Even in that very short time I tried to give Dung a hint that saying too much would hurt him, but I had to speak in parables. I had no idea whether Dung was smart enough to read them. I pointed out to him, "A frog that makes too much noise will die," and I hoped he understood my secret message: that the more you confess, the more they will enquire and the more you will be tortured and may even die.

Tragically, events showed that although poor Dung may have been well trained as a soldier and served in the best division of the Vietnamese army, he was not a reader of riddles and definitely not a strategist who could prepare what he was to say to the Khmer Rouge.

As I predicted, three days later Boong Chian, Oum Uot and others arrived. I did not see Dhara in this group, but I knew Dung was about to undergo ferocious torture nonetheless. At first he refused to talk, and I heard the interpreter shouting in Vietnamese. I heard blows, the screams of pain from electric shocks, the hiccups from being kicked from the front and the voice from a plastic bag.

"If you are not going to talk, these soldiers will continue bashing you," the interpreter shouted. I knew Dung was tough, but toughness was not the answer when you were in the hands of professional killers.

A couple of days later, Boong Chian took me to see Dung. His face was swollen and bruised, his hands were bound behind his back and his legs were pulled and tied apart, just as mine had been. The bamboo they had used to torture Thanh was lying there. It was hard for me to see my fellow soldier this way.

I thank God they did not force me to torture Dung. What could I have done if they had compelled me to act in that way? But tough Dung had made those soldiers tired, and they left for the day.

The pain of the first day one can bear, but if they carry out the torture on the same person, in the same spot, day after day, then pain is doubled and tripled in its effect. Dung soon gave up and spoke. He only knew a little, for he was a new soldier who had come directly from Vietnam a few months before.

Dung was chained in exactly the same place as Thanh, and I feared he would die in the same awful way. But somehow he survived. He was later released by the intervention of the International Red Cross at the same time as I was. Now he lives in Canada, but I have lost contact with him. Sadly, his ordeal damaged his judgment and he is no longer totally sound in his mind.

Chapter fifteen

THAI MILITARY PRISON

The day the Khmer Rouge freed me from their hell, I had no warning. It was in the early weeks of 1985, and I was set free, along with Dung, thanks to the intervention of the International Red Cross.

The morning began like any other except that on this day Boong Chian and another unfamiliar soldier came to me. They swung their AK-47s onto their backs and stood looking at me, hands resting on their hips. The new soldier delivered a short message: "*A Uong, tau Bangkok*. Uong, you go to Bangkok." Chian took a key and began to unchain my feet.

Remembering Minh, I knew that the term *tau Bangkok* was a euphemism for execution and death. *This is it!* I thought. *This is my day, and I am willing to accept my fate.* My heart beat faster as fear took hold, although I had been prepared for death for a long time.

Should I beg them for mercy? It would not work with these people. Minh and Thanh had begged, but their lives had ended even while they were begging. *I will not plead with them*, I thought, and decided to accept whatever fate came to me. How would I die? I didn't know, but there was a sense of regret that I would not live to keep my promise to my mother. I knew I could change nothing in this situation, but if they killed me, my wish was that it would be in the same way they killed Minh, not how they killed Thanh. A bullet through the back of the head was the honorable thing I wished for, and then I would be forever gone from the face of the earth.

But *tau Bangkok* seemed to be true for us that day. The soldiers took Dung and me from that death camp along a pathway to a less dense area of the jungle. We were both very weak and had no energy to run—Dung could not even walk properly—and our eyes were blindfolded. Our hands were bound as usual, but not behind us like before. Although I could see nothing, I could feel the pathway was getting wider, with less grass and fewer trees. There were fewer singing birds and insects. I could even feel, under my feet, that the road was smoother and had been used for oxcarts.

How long, and for what distance, we walked on that road I have no idea. But around mid-afternoon we were led onto a concrete road, and there I heard a group of people speaking to one another, not in Khmer but a different language. I guessed it must be Thai. The soldiers removed our blindfolds and we saw six people: the two Khmer Rouge soldiers in their green uniforms, three Thai soldiers and one Red Cross representative. They spoke together in Thai, or perhaps in English, but I had no idea what they were talking about. Then they pointed us to a pickup truck about ten meters away.

The Khmer Rouge soldiers retreated and the Red Cross representative climbed into the cabin of the pickup. The Thai soldiers blindfolded us again before we sped away.

I did not know where we were going, and I did not know anybody to ask. I did not even bother to ask. Wherever they took us, whatever they intended to do with us, we had no choice anyway.

One thing I was sure about was that I was now in a more civilized place, and within Thai territory. As the pickup truck accelerated, I knew I was escaping my death chamber forever. It was almost too good to be true. Surely these people would lead us to a better place. Yet fear had not totally evaporated. Experience was telling me that I would not be loved, or even liked, by the Thai soldiers. If I was in safe hands, why was I still blindfolded?

The truck drove very fast—I had never traveled in such a fast vehicle in my life. With my eyes blindfolded, I could not see anything or enjoy the Thai landscape, but the wind blew in where we sat. It had taken me from 1983 to early 1985 to cross that border from Cambodia into Thailand.

Quite late in the afternoon, we arrived at our destination. The truck slowed down and stopped. We were unloaded and the blindfolds were removed.

The first sight that met our eyes was a two-story building in a compound, with barbed wire around it and military guards at the gate. It must have been late because a unit of Thai soldiers were preparing their dinner. Another group stood nearby with their AR-15 rifles in their hands. It was the first time I had encountered Thai soldiers face-to-face. I had seen them and their movements through my binoculars before, but now they were up close, watching me. They saluted the men who had brought us from the border, so these must have been higher ranking soldiers. Language differences prevented me from understanding their conversation, but somehow, in my gut, I knew I was not safe yet.

These military men and the intelligence service will squeeze me for every piece of army information again, I thought. I had to be very watchful in this new territory.

As the gates opened allowing us into the compound, I saw that behind the three-meter-high barbed wire fence was a whole group of Thai prisoners with chains on their feet. Their eyes displayed hostility. Now I knew I was in another prison. "Have I fallen out of the frying pan into the fire?" I asked myself, and willed myself to be more cautious.

Eventually we were led inside the building—the first time I had been inside any building for a very long time. I was able to see and try to talk with Dung. His face was green like a young leaf in the jungle, and his eyes were sunken in their sockets and displayed no life. His cheek bones protruded and were very pale. I could not imagine how any person could be paler or weaker. Of course, I could not see my own face, because I had not looked in a mirror since I was captured by the Khmer Rouge.

Dung could not walk properly—his movements were as clumsy as those of a tottering baby. He stood up and fell again. Instinctively I reached my arm towards him in the hope of catching him before he hit the concrete floor. Just as my hand touched Dung, a sharp pain exploded in my right shoulder and I was knocked down.

Out of nowhere, a guard with a long club had hit me with all his strength. I quickly looked up and saw a big soldier with blazing eyes lifting the club to strike another blow. I could not avoid it. *Thwack!* This time I thought my shoulder must be broken because I did not have much physical condition left after many months in captivity.

He swore in Thai and an interpreter, somewhere out of sight, swore in Vietnamese. "You ——! You must not give help anybody in here. If you do, the Thai will kick you to death."

We were shoved towards the second floor stairs, accompanied by a mouthful from the Vietnamese translator, who I later learned was named Trung. He swore every second word. "You ——, get up there!" Both Dung and I had been in chains for a long time and had undergone severe torture; it was hard for us to walk fast, let alone climb a staircase. Dung was falling down, but I wasn't allowed to help him. It was humiliating for me to be unable to give a hand to a person who was almost crippled.

The swearing continued from Trung. "Walk faster! Move faster! If you do not go up fast, the Thai soldiers will punish you more. They will kick you to death."

Death! I had heard that threatening word many times before and now I had to hear it again. I had no understanding of the Thai language, but the term 'death' led me to expect another show of brutality.

I was still able to move at a reasonable pace, but Dung was not. His knees had been hammered for a long time. He literally crawled up the staircase with tears running down from his sunken eyes, his arm waving at me, his voice pleading with me for help: "*Đồng hương!* My countryman!" These were the first words he had ever spoken to me. In the Khmer Rouge camp he had only looked at me, perhaps thinking I was a deserter and could not be trusted.

My emotions rose and I reached out to help him. I received another blow. The Thai soldiers were right there, laughing at our humiliation. I did not know what to think, so I moved upward and waited for Dung at the top of the stairs.

On the second floor, in one huge cell behind iron bars, I saw many other young Vietnamese men, all half-naked with only boxer shorts on. They too were soldiers. They had watched us moving slowly up the stairs. One or two swore and shouted, "*Lại hai em nữa!* Another two men!" but most greeted us warmly. From their second-floor barred windows they could see what was going on at the gate and had seen our arrival.

Meeting people who could speak our language was a real joy to me. I felt like jumping on them and embracing them as comrades. But this joy was short-lived, because I found later that most of them were deserters who had crossed the border into Thailand in search of a better life, as Minh and Thanh had tried to do.

I was just about to open my mouth to speak when Trung shouted to the other inmates in the hall, "These two are *Bắc Kỳ* (a derogatory term for Northerners); make them room near the toilet." Near the toilet! I had slept on my own excrement for many months, so to be near the toilet did not worry me. I had never been in prison with so many others, and the luxury of a toilet was something beyond my thinking. I didn't care where I slept; any place that had a roof and a toilet was still a thousand times better than the Khmer Rouge prison where there was no roof and no toilet.

We were tired and slept well that night.

The next day the inmates started to ply us with questions. "Where is your hometown?" someone asked Dung. Others wanted to know where his unit was stationed in Cambodia and what his real task was.

Dung's mind was almost gone, but he never lost the knowledge of his identity. With his North Central accent he replied, "*Tôi ở quê bác* . . . I am from Nam Đàn, the birthplace of Uncle Ho, and I am from Division 308 stationed in Ta-Cuong."

I could not stop him in time. Now it was too late. I heard a few swear words in the crowd, a snarl and mocking laugher, as though these young soldiers now had nothing to do with the army or Ho Chi Minh, and no pride in their Vietnamese identity.

Word went out fast thanks to some loose-lipped volunteer informants. Trung, the interpreter, came with a Thai officer in the afternoon, and Dung and I were called to the cell gate. As we approached, Trung pointed at us and declared to the guards, "These are true Viet Cong from North Vietnam."

I saw the officer's face change fast. He opened the gate, strode two steps towards us and, with his big hands, grasped Dung's neck and my shoulder. He said something in anger then forcefully pushed us into a small cell separate from the main room.

"Viet Cong must stay in this cell," Trung translated.

With walls of bars and no toilet, the cell was like a little pigeonhole. The disadvantage of it was that we had to ask permission for everything, from extra water to going to relieve ourselves. With sickness and malaria still attacking us often, the confined space gave us even more difficulty. Still, it was much better than the Khmer Rouge camp.

The problem was only heightened a couple of weeks later when six other Vietnamese soldiers, this time from Laos, were put into our three-meter-square living area with us. We slept by top-and-tailing so we would all fit.

One cell mate, a man named Hòa from Thanh Hóa province, often woke me in the middle of the night and whispered, "Are you okay?" I calmly assured him I was fine. After this happened several times I said, "Why do you have to ask me that question so many times?"

"Because your body is always so cold when you sleep. You are as cold as a dead person, and you sleep so quietly. I have to wake you to find out if you are dead or alive."

After Hòa's comment I started to observe my body. What he said was true. Every night when I slept, I sweated a lot and my whole body became as cold as a dead body.

A few days after we arrived at the prison, known as Aranjapathet Military Camp, Trung ran up the stairs to call our names. "You two *Bắc Kỳ*, come down to see the officers."

We were led down to the basement of the building. If we had still been with the other inmates in the main cell, we would have been warned about this new development. But because we were separated in *Chuồng Cu*, our tiny pigeonhole, we had no idea of what was to come.

In the basement we were led into a special room. On one side was a big cabinet holding chains of various sizes. A Thai officer was sitting at a table in the middle of the room. He regarded us with a fierce look. He was big, dark, and almost twice my size, and spoke with a deep, powerful voice as if to scare us. Through Trung he told us he was the highest ranking officer in the facility and wanted us to tell him the whole truth.

"The truth is the only thing we accept here," he warned. "If it's not the truth," his left hand picked up a dark brown club about sixty centimeters long and three or four centimeters thick, "this will not spare you."

He lifted a fat finger to point at me, signifying I would be the first to be interrogated. As I came near the table, I sat down on an empty chair I thought was for me. In Vietnamese culture, it is polite to place both hands on the table when talking to any older or higher-ranked person. As I placed my hands on the desk, the officer became so furious that he struck both my arms with his club, very hard.

He half stood up and shouted, then Trung shouted and swore the translation: "Who allowed you to sit? And who allowed you to put those filthy hands on my desk?"

I looked at Trung instinctively, and another few blows hit my shoulder. Trung shouted the translation again: "Why do you turn to the interpreter?"

I did not know what to do, but then a quick thought came to my mind: *This Thai will intimidate you to get every single piece of information about the Vietnamese army he can.* But I had been through this before, and I knew he would not get anything from me. "I'm not like the deserters he has been treating with contempt," I told myself. I started to call up my old defense strategy immediately: lying to live, and lying logically, consistently.

The officer looked directly at me and started asking questions. His hand remained firmly on the club and he used it at will. Another officer in the corner wrote down every answer I gave, whether true or false. Now it was not the torturer I feared, but the man with the pen who recorded everything. With notes they could compare information and identify inconsistencies in my confession. A single illogical statement would be thought of as lying. I would be bashed again and again until they were satisfied. The Thais were much better equipped to note inconsistencies than the Khmer Rouge, who never recorded anything. They only bashed and bashed.

Despite this new apprehension, I was encouraged by one thing. I could see that the Thai interrogator, although harsh, was aiming merely to intimidate me to get information. All the blows he unleashed were directed at my arm and shoulder, so I concluded this bashing would not end in death. Of course, those who had deserted from the army would fear him and pass on everything they knew to avoid being hurt. But I said to myself, "He will only get the information I learnt by heart for the Khmer Rouge." And I would leave no trace that I was lying to him.

After about an hour of this ordeal, I stopped him and calmly called the interpreter's name. "Trung! Can you tell the officer that I have been in a Khmer Rouge prison for almost two years and that all my information will be out of date and useless to him anyway!"

The officer shouted and struck me again for interrupting his questioning. However, Trung translated what I had said to him. The officer looked at me in surprise. I received a few more blows to my lower shoulder, but that was the last of it that day.

Dung was the next victim. I could scarcely bear to sit three meters away and witness such beating and swearing. It went for more than two hours. Dung's mind had almost gone, and it seemed he had little to say beyond stating his personal identity and the fact that he was one of the soldiers in the best division of the Vietnamese army. His words had no logic, no consistency. The worst beating came when he was asked about his activities in the army. Dung declared, "Soldiers in my unit never considered the Thai Army, or any army, as any concern. We would cross into Thai territory at will. We came many times."

At this the officer stood up—the first time I had seen him react that way—and started raining blows on Dung's head and shoulders. Dung merely bent his head, as though there was no pain, or he had simply spoken a fact. I did not understand why he said such things to the interrogator despite many heavy blows. And I could not decide whether the officer was truly searching for information or just vengefully punishing Dung for what he had automatically said.

I attempted to tell the officer that Dung's mind had gone, so it was pointless interrogating him. But there was no room for debate in that room.

The bashings gave us an uncomfortable night. Whichever side I tried to roll onto brought intense pain, particularly in both shoulders. But tiredness gave way to sleep anyway.

Those of us in the pigeonhole had to live and eat at the same pace as the other prisoners, as dictated by the guards. It was never easy. Although our legs were chained, we were made to run fast up and down the stairs. We had to exercise the same as other prisoners. Often we had to take our clothes off and bathe naked in the time it took the guards to count from one to ten. Or we had to sit down and eat our whole meal by the time they counted to ten. Thank God they did not give us a lot of food, and we never wore any underwear to complicate the process of undressing over the leg chains. Otherwise we would have been subjected to more punishment.

Two weeks after we arrived at Aranjapathet, we were called to be investigated by the TOMI (Thai Organization of Military Intelligence). Their office was about 30 minutes' drive from the prison. The officials there were much nicer, but I had heard they even used lie detectors to determine whether a person was telling the truth or not, and I was nervous how such a machine would measure my confession. Fortunately, I never had to face that test.

The interpreter in this office was named Phong, and he was more mature and cultured than Trung (a farmer from the Mekong Delta). Phong was a chemical engineer who had been trained in Russia and sent to Cambodia to see how chemical weapons were used against Vietnamese soldiers. I did not know why he had escaped or how he came to be collaborating with the Thai army.

Phong did not speak Thai but used English instead. He spoke with a soft voice, indicating he was different from the previous interpreters I had to deal with. It also showed that he had a higher level of intelligence. I thought he would surely know more about the life of a soldier and the activities of the Vietnamese army in Cambodia than the rest of the deserters in Aranjapathet. This increased my fear of being detected for lying.

I was called into an office with Phong. Two officers were

waiting, one a Thai and the other of Western appearance. I had to try very hard to swallow my fear, exercise self-control and prime my defense mechanism.

"Please sit down," Phong invited me, pointing to a stool. I had not come across this kind of language and gesture for years.

Phong was free to talk to me as the other two observed. They asked about many details of the battle I was involved in, along with my rank and the nature of my work. I answered them exactly as I had answered the Khmer Rouge before. I also told them I had been in Khmer Rouge captivity for almost two years and had no up-to-date information. Therefore there was no point in asking me about the Vietnamese army's tactics.

Thank God this strategy worked again. I was discharged from their presence. Because they truly knew I had come from a Khmer Rouge prison, they realized there was no point in digging for useless information.

Dung was called in, but the TOMI people did not abuse or torture him. They looked at his bearing and realized he was not mentally competent. They released us both early that day. Before we left the office, Phong handed each of us a bag containing two pairs of underwear, two Crocodile T-shirts, and two packs of Samith cigarettes (a special Thai brand). Every Vietnamese soldier who came to TOMI had the privilege of selling his information for that price, and, of course, those who were deserters shared freely. For me, the safety of my army comrades and my honor as a soldier could not be so violated; but I accepted the bag of clothes and especially the cigarettes anyway. I needed them badly.

We were returned to our pigeonhole where I could sell the undies for about 16 baht each, or trade them for more cigarettes with the Thai soldiers. There was no point in wearing them anyway. In prison, cigarettes were the most valuable thing. I would never sell them. I needed them to keep me warm and satisfied.

Chapter sixteen

INTO THE REFUGEE CAMP

———————————

M arch 20, 1985 marked one of the happiest days of my life. International Red Cross personnel came to visit the Thai prisoners quite often, but not the eight of us in the pigeonhole because the Thai officers hid us away. Yet somehow a rumor had reached us that on this day in March many would be sent to Phanat Nikhom refugee camp. Where did the prisoners get that information? I had no idea, but we all waited to see.

"In Phanat Nikhom we can work, go out, study," we speculated. "There will be no more lining up, no more bashing, cursing, abusing." Wow! We had been mistreated and half-starved, deprived of our basic human rights and subjected to all kinds of suppression in this military prison, so to think about a place with freedom, good food, and a normal life revived our will to live. We were excited.

All the prisoners dreamed of being treated with respect, but especially Dung and me. We had not been treated as human beings for a very long time. To the Khmer Rouge we were less than animals, and in Aranjapathet we were considered worse than criminals, separated in a tiny cell and viewed differently from the other Vietnamese inmates. Our deep desire was to be free. We wondered when and how we would leave our dungeon. To us a refugee camp was an idyllic place full of nice things. We had never seen one, yet this hope gave us something to dream about. And the dream kept us alive.

The morning finally came. The inmates on the second floor

peered through the windows to see if there were any signs of transport vehicles coming. "I see a bus!" one person shouted with excitement. All the inmates rushed to the window to see for themselves. Even those of us in the pigeonhole stood on tiptoe even though we could see nothing clearly. Our ears listened to hear whether a transport vehicle had truly arrived.

Someone turned from the window and said, "I saw the bus stop at the gate!" He took a deep breath then added, "And I saw a couple of people in civilian clothes get out!" The whole atmosphere changed rapidly. Everyone clapped their hands; we were all so excited. And why not? Hope had become reality.

Before long I heard a soldier's footsteps on the stairs. He swore at the prisoners, but then he unlocked the gate and flung it open. All the prisoners were called down to the garden to meet the International Red Cross personnel. They helped them line up in order, and then read out the names of those who would be allowed to go to Phanat Nikhom camp in Thailand's southern Chonburi Province.

Many had gone down to the garden. Many were called. Even our six cell mates from the pigeonhole were gone. But Dung and I were left behind. Dung had not been thinking clearly for a while, yet seeing what was going on below caused him great distress. I could see the disappointment and frustration written on his face. I was also very concerned, but I could conceal my anxiety as if nothing was happening.

"Why didn't they call us?" Dung asked, bewildered. "So many of them came here after me, but look, now they're all lined up, smiling, and waiting for the bus to take them off to this dream camp."

I gestured to him to be quiet and wait, but my own mind was burning with questions. What would happen to us? Were we going to continue to be subjected to this suppression? How long would we have to stay here? My heart was racing, still hoping to hear our names called. It was Ho Chi Minh who said, "One day in prison is equal to a thousand years outside," and I had proven him right. I had been held in military prisons and subjected to ill-treatment for too long. I wanted to see life in a better place, and anywhere was better than this pigeonhole.

After everyone had lined up ready to board the bus, the Red Cross representative walked over to the officers and exchanged some words. It looked like a serious conversation. Five or ten minutes later, Trung ran up the staircase. He inserted the key into the pigeonhole's lock and shouted, "You ——, better dress and get out of here. The bus is waiting!'

I had never seen Dung move so fast before; he had his shirt on in about one second. No wonder he was in a special army unit. We ran down the stairs to the basement as if we had wings, despite the chains still between our legs. Then we anxiously waited for the prison officers to free us from them. Every minute of delay was too long to endure, for we were afraid we might miss the bus. *Clang, clang, clang!* With a few professional hammer strokes, the warden bent the rings that chained our ankles.

Trung led us to the bus. I walked with my head down, humbly. I had to make sure I was not seen to be acting in defiance of the warden. I did not want to cause any suspicion and make the Thai guards change their minds about our freedom. At the bus, our names were crossed off and we boarded.

The bus revved its engine, rolled its wheels, and slowly moved off, working through the gears. As I looked back at the building surrounded by barbed wire, I raised my hand and found myself whispering, "Goodbye, prison, goodbye."

The Khmer Rouge camp was about life and death, the Thai prison was about indifference, but Phanat Nikhom refugee camp was about despair, desperation and depression. I was in the camp from 1985 to 1989. The months and years dragged along, taking the best part of life with them. Yes, we were freer than before, but that didn't mean there was an absence of violence.

As soon as we set foot in the camp, we were led to an area designated for ex-soldiers only. Once again we were behind barbed wire. Much to his dismay, Trung, the Thai prison interpreter, who had come with us to Phanat Nikhom, was left with us. He thought he would be treated differently by the Thai authorities, but he wasn't. He was now a dumped card.

Many other Aran guys (the term we used for ex-military

prisoners from Aranjapathet) were already living in Phanat Nikhom. They had heard rumors of recent abuse and ill-treatment of prisoners at Aranjapathet, and they were waiting for Trung and his cohorts for vengeance.

As soon as we arrived, we were all ushered into a large hall, and some of the self-proclaimed leaders forced Trung and the others to stand up in front of us. They demanded answers. The questions were ones Trung had never been asked and was unprepared to answer.

"We were all seeking freedom, so why did you take advantage of these people?"

There was anger and loathing in their voices. Those standing up with Trung were only his followers; it was he, the man who spoke Thai, the man who collaborated with the Thais, who had caused all the trouble. Now he stood alone. His cronies would be punished, but it was Trung who was truly despised.

The leaders asked everyone who had been abused in Aran to line up and pay him back. Many punched him, others kicked and a few slapped his face. Now it was Trung who had to bear all the hatred. Many were quite happy to deliver this with their fists. Trung had a poor manner and a foul mouth, but this mob was no better. It was all about who had the upper hand, and there was no justice in this sort of action.

Seeing the revenge being meted out in full force, I was really shocked. Was this the dream camp we had so anticipated?

When it was almost my turn, I quietly told Dung, "We're not going to bash this guy; we have nothing to do with this mob." Dung saw me refuse to beat Trung, so he also declined to do so. Many of those in the line behind me followed suit.

My heart went out to Trung because he was just a victim of foolish and naïve thinking. The ironic thing was that no one stood by him. Where were all his friends from Aranjapathet? Where were his former supporters and informants? Not a single person dared to stand up for him. His old friends, whose mouths were so foul, said nothing on his behalf. Trung must have been very surprised by how fickle and feeble they were. As a result, he never integrated into the group in Phanat Nikhom. He later became involved with a

Laotian girl and moved permanently to Site Two with the Laotian community. I think he was broken-hearted.

Phanat Nikhom in reality was never a dream camp for us. Even though we could cook our own food and live a more normal life, it was still a refugee camp. For a start, we were separated from the civilians in the camp. A barbed wire boundary divided us, even though we were all Vietnamese. We were free to move between sections of the camp to make friends and look for relatives, and we could also find manual jobs outside our section, but the ex-soldiers had to live apart from everyone else. There were often clashes between the civilians (mainly those who had served in the old South Vietnamese regime) and us Communist ex-soldiers. This was the result of people carrying emotional garbage from the old days. I found it ridiculous and childish, repeating the vicious cycle of hatred and vengeance.

In Phanat Nikhom most of us faced another obstacle. The majority of ex-soldiers were the sons of poor farmers and had little education, so they had no desire to study. For me, learning English seemed good preparation for future resettlement in a third country, but to many it was too hard. Good organizations came to help us in the camp, but a lot of ex-soldiers failed to see it. They preferred to learn Thai and find jobs as shop assistants, earning a little hard cash and feeling good about it. They only had a short-term vision. I tried to encourage them to focus on a longer-term vision: "Don't you see that many of the nations that open their doors to accept refugees are English-speaking, like Canada, America, Australia, England and New Zealand?" They all saw it, but it was just too difficult for them to apply themselves. "English is too hard!" they said. Perhaps, having been in combat units in Cambodia, they were all too traumatized, too emotionally unsettled and too psychologically damaged, to be able to pursue anything academic.

Being different from most people in the camp, I focused on learning English, despite its being hard. I tried because I could not see any other way out. I had not intended to escape from the army, but I was there in this camp and had automatically become a refugee. An opportunity had opened for me and I grasped it with all my capacity. Many times I felt frustrated and wanted to give up learning, but as a disciplined young man I kept on with the challenge. One of my incentives to learn English was that I had read books by Mark Twain and several other great English writers in translation. I had also heard Dad talking highly about Shakespeare. I had a desire to one day read those wonderful writers in their own language.

I wanted an English–Vietnamese dictionary to help me expand my English vocabulary, but to buy one I needed money. There weren't many jobs in the camp, but that did not deter me from looking for one. I would ask anyone who looked like they had money to hire me to do something, anything. And I never minded telling them my purpose in earning the money.

One day a friend who knew of my desire introduced me to a man who had extended family living in America. They sent money to him regularly.

"He needs a job," my friend said, pointing at me. "You can hire him to draw water for you. Just pay him a little. He needs cigarettes and a dictionary to learn English."

"Learn English?" The man looked at me as though he had just heard something funny.

"He's an ex-soldier and lives in Side B. He can take water from the tank at the end of the camp to fill your container," my friend urged.

The man began to act like a boss. He looked me over from head to toe with a suspicious stare. Knowing I was a Northerner from my accent, and an ex-soldier, seemed to excite him. He smirked from the left side of his mouth. I guess he had some thought of vengeance, or was amused by my name and my willingness to work for so little money. He nodded to my friend.

"All right," he told me, "I'll hire you to draw eight buckets of water for my family, every morning at 8.00 am, right after the Thai national anthem." He then added clearly the price he was willing to pay. "I'll give you 10 baht every week."

Ten baht per week! That was a lot of money to me. It was actually worth about 40 Australian cents, but to someone who had never earned much money before, it seemed marvelous. As a boy at home, I had no idea about money. Whatever I made I gave to my mother to help with the family. In the army, we only received our pay every three months, or even every six months, and we could spend all those little Vietnamese dong and Cambodian riel in a few days on sweets, cigarettes, alcohol and parties.

Ten baht is good money, I thought, imagining that within three months I could buy the coveted dictionary. "Deal," I agreed. "Can I start tomorrow morning?"

He nodded again and showed me his house, with a large concrete water tank sitting nearby.

Working and dreaming made me forget about the miserable life of the past and the frustrations of the present. After three months of work and saving, I bought both a bi-lingual dictionary and a little Oxford English dictionary, with 12,000 entries. These were my first personal possessions in life, and I treasured them highly. I intended to learn all the words in them by heart, and dreamed of speaking English well enough to have conversations with native speakers and devour the works of Shakespeare and other English literary heroes.

Having a dictionary and a desire to master the language helped me set aside everything and focus on one thing: learning English. I studied all the time, mostly till past midnight, memorizing and rewriting new vocabulary. I learnt the little Oxford dictionary by heart in a few months. But, to my dismay, I found that learning vocabulary alone was not enough. I needed to know more about structure and how to use the language and make sense in conversation. Many foreigners were available in the camp who spoke English, so I decided to ask for help.

Jim, Janet, Gale, and Thomas were just four of the many volunteer workers from America whom I only remember by their first names. They helped shape my spoken English. But the person I remember the most was Rebecca Henry, a nurse from New York and a woman with a great heart. She assisted me with my English while I did voluntary work alongside her for the American Refugee Committee. In learning English, I also came to understand more about my new American friends. They were not all demons, arrogant or imperialistic as I had been taught by Communist propaganda. As a matter of fact, many of the Americans I met were very humble, very generous, and willing to help with all their hearts. I was deeply touched by them. (Of course, there were wonderful people in the camp from other nationalities as well.)

As the months passed, with hard work and a desire to practice and master the language, I began to be able to hold sensible conversations with friends who were not Vietnamese. It was then that I realized I needed to contribute as a volunteer worker in the camp. Now that my English was good enough, I took on the role of interpreter.

My desire to assist in this way opened many doors for me. One door was a deeper understanding of my own people and the reason why many had escaped from Vietnam. Being an interpreter for the International Red Cross, Thai Red Cross and the camp's social workers, I became more aware of the perils my own people had undergone. Few of them had wanted to leave their homes; they were driven away broken-hearted by their ill-treatment at the hands of different regimes. Political hardship in the Communist utopia, re-education camps, New Economic Zones, education bias and economic stupidity had made them flee. Many had lost everything, including homes, savings and family members, before they decided to leave in search of freedom and something better than the Communist state.

After they fled, many, like Minh and Thanh, lost their lives in the Cambodian jungles. Many more were lost at sea, or were attacked in the Gulf of Thailand by fishermen whom greed had turned into deadly pirates. The years 1986 and 1987 had the highest numbers of Vietnamese boat people. Almost every day hundreds arrived in Thailand and ended up in Phanat Nikhom. At one time, the tiny camp held around 20,000 people.

It took me a while to fully appreciate the pain of the refugees. As an assistant to the social workers, I was sent out to greet new arrivals. As the Red Cross interpreter, I heard about countless missing relatives and family members. I heard countless stories of hardship on the journey to Thailand. Countless young women reported being raped. Large numbers arrived having lost their entire families. I was there in the office helping with the translation process and saw it all.

My life journey had been a tough one, but through hearing the stories of my own people, God made my heart softer. The tears of my people soaked the soil of the camp. Sometimes I felt crushed by all the reports. I was no longer a proud Communist soldier. The Lord was leading me through all of this to understand not only others, but also myself.

Life is transient in a refugee camp, with people coming and going daily. In our ex-soldiers' section, many were accepted by countries such as France, Scandinavia, the USA and Canada. As time went by, many of those who had come to the camp with me also left. But to us, a group of captured soldiers from the 'North,' the chance to go anywhere remained slim. We seemed to be forgotten. Maybe the world outside didn't even know we existed. I could bury myself in my volunteer work and study, but others could not.

Among the Vietnamese who had resettled in America and Australia were some who dreamed of recapturing Vietnam. Their hope of overthrowing the Communist government through violence was real. Some secretly came back to the camp to recruit young people to repatriate to Vietnam and wage guerrilla warfare. They called their goal *Phục Quốc* ('recovering the nation').

One day, after a hard day's work, I learnt that two of my friends, Binh and Ban, had enlisted to go back and fight in the jungle again. I was furious. They had come to the camp much later than I had, but they could not handle the frustration of waiting for resettlement. I ran to confront the young men in their room.

"You idiots!" I yelled. "Why did you decide to repatriate without consulting anybody? What hope is there in these organizations that you're willing to go and fight for? You have no idea who they are and what they can do to help you find a future!"

They were shocked at my behavior, partly because they had never seen an outburst like it before, and partly because I was, stupidly, lecturing them in front of other people.

Binh was a stubborn man from North Central Vietnam, and he felt real shame at being castigated publicly. It was a loss of face. He became very emotional and very angry.

"Shut up, Uong! Shut up!" he swore, his face red and his

fist rolled into a ball. "You go to school and learn and hope to be resettled in other countries, but look at you! Just look at you! You're working for three organizations, you can speak English, but what good has it done you? The Dutch called you up and rejected you on the spot. The Americans promised never to accept you. Where are you going, huh?"

I was stunned at the way he shot back at me and couldn't find words to answer him.

"Where are YOU going?" He shouted even louder to emphasize his point. "You're one of the best in here and yet you have no hope, so what about us?"

By now Binh had lost control. He was screaming louder and louder, his saliva hitting me in the face. He had always been very self-controlled and respected, and he was quite fond of me. But this time he could not hold his tongue. Desperation and despair had made him lose hope of being resettled anywhere in the world.

He had scored his point and it pierced my heart.

"But you'll go back and fight against your family and your countrymen!" I shouted back at him. "Do you think the Vietnamese army, with all those experienced fighters, will allow you to reach them? You'll die a pointless death!"

By this time the others in the room were leaving to cool things down.

Looking back now, I deeply regret the way I challenged my soldier friends that day. I should have been more professional and patient while probing the issues. If I had shown more reasoning skill, respecting them rather than shouting at them, it may have helped persuade them to reject the lie of repatriation. My exasperation only made matters worse. The shouting went on for some time, but it only entrenched the differences between us. Binh, Ban and the others who had signed up dug in with their decision to sneak out of the camp and return to Vietnam.

I could not reason with them, and frankly I had little heart for it. I myself had also almost lost patience after waiting for more than two years and being rejected by the Dutch delegation. No other country was interested in us.

A few weeks after the argument with Binh and the others, a

Canadian delegation came to the camp. They called me in for an interview. Henry, a representative of the UNHCR (United Nations High Commissioner for Refugees), introduced me. The interviewer, a man named Paul, looked through my five different résumés and recommendations from the various organizations I had worked with. He then conducted a long interview with me through an interpreter.

Towards the end of the interview he asked, "Do you speak English?"

I politely replied, "Yes, I do."

"Tell me about your life, your birthplace, where you come from."

"I am from Thanh Hóa province," I replied, exactly as I had told the Khmer Rouge and the Thai TOMI.

"Where's that?"

"It is in North Vietnam."

His face and gestures immediately changed. "North Vietnam?" he repeated in a high-pitched voice. He threw himself back in his chair.

I asked Xuan, the interpreter, to explain my birthplace to him, but I knew something was wrong. My confidence drained away. Paul stopped speaking to me in English and went back to speaking through Xuan. He indicated I needed to leave the room so he could discuss with others in the delegation the issue of my birthplace.

After the door shut behind me, I knew they would reject me, just as the Dutch delegation had previously. Fifteen minutes of waiting dragged by. Finally Xuan came out. "Uong!" he called with a wave. "You can come in."

Paul sat relaxing, his back on the chair. Through Xuan he conveyed their verdict. Basically, the Canadian delegation had come to the conclusion that they could not allow a North Vietnamese soldier onto their soil. Although I had many recommendations from the organizations I had worked with, and although I had proven I was a person of worth, they cold-heartedly rejected my case on the grounds that I was born in North Vietnam.

I had faced rejection before, but this seemed too much for me. I stood there dripping sweat, speechless and motionless. The feeling was very much like the time I was surprised by the Khmer Rouge in the dry streambed in Cambodia. My heart, my whole being, was frozen.

Paul stared at me defiantly in a way I will never forget. It was the stare of someone who had the authority to accept a wounded soul or reject it; to let him into his group or kick him out into the darkness. He moved his left hand in a gesture for me to leave the room; he and his delegation wanted to continue their interviews.

After hearing I had been rejected by the Canadian delegation, Khun Saroj, the social worker, took me to her office to console me, along with Khun Naowarat, the chief UN representative. Mr Leo, the Danish head of the UNHCR office in Phanat Nikhom, also came to give support. He gave me a promise: "Don't worry too much. The Danish may come at the end of the year, and I will intervene for you. They will accept you. I know you are a good person."

It was good counsel, and the right promise at the right time. But I struggled to go home to share my humiliation with Dung and my other friends. It would also be harder to face the guys who had registered their names to repatriate to Vietnam. The Canadian rejection would be evidence to push them even further in their belief that in Phanat Nikhom there was no hope for any of us. My anger at Binh and Ban had been pointless.

I found myself becoming increasingly angry with the overseas Vietnamese who bribed their way into the camp to lure such naive young men back into the jungle and ultimately to their deaths. Some of these organizations were run by ex-officers of the old South Vietnamese regime, who after resettling had the time, money and ambition to use these new victims for their belligerent and delusional power games. But these young men needed support, not abuse; they needed guidance, not manipulation. We needed people of the older generation to teach us about the ways of the world out there, not to lure us back into the vicious cycle of fighting and devouring each other. Cowards were people who had no courage to accept the truth that their time had passed. The day of their power was gone; there was no way to get it back. What they were doing was nothing more than perpetuating the horror of war, struggle and death, with more victims, more refugees.

To me, no other delegation was crueler or more cold-hearted than the Canadians at that crucial moment in our lives. With their mock humanitarian program and indifferent decisions that day, they did not help us at all. Later on, after I left the camp for Australia, I was informed that Binh and the others had died in the Cambodian jungle. This news increased my sense of bitterness.

Chapter seventeen

A SEARCHING HEART

I had never been a religious person before, but after being in the Khmer Rouge death camp, then in the Thai military prison, and now being rejected twice by two delegations, bitter disappointment was driving me to think more deeply. I was 26 years old, an age when I felt I should show more maturity and search more for understanding and 'truth'. I began wondering more about life.

Many times I looked at Dung and saw how this once brave soldier was now a simple man, made silly by torture and imprisonment. I felt sorry for him. *Why Dung?* I wondered. *Why Minh and Thanh?* Two were dead and one was now almost an invalid, but I was still alive. The line of thought continued: *So many people I've translated for in this camp are unfortunate. Is there any meaning behind all these things? What is my purpose in living anyway?*

As a translator for the social workers in the camp, I knew almost everyone there. One way or another, they had all undergone crisis and were now faced with more. In the Thai military prison I had learnt the painful truth that in times of need, hunger, thirst and deprivation, people will show their real selves. The character of a man will be revealed during suppression or crisis. I was now bored to death because all I had seen in this camp was disorder and people focusing on the short-term. Something very surreal was happening to them, yet it had little effect on moving them to make what should have been a long-term investment. In the refugee camp I saw people fight for as little as a handful of rice, a liter of water, or a small fish. Why shouldn't they anyway?

As I was learning English, I got to the point where I was capable of conducting small, meaningful conversations with others. Rebecca Henry, my colleague at the American Refugee Committee, saw I enjoyed reading, so she gave me my first English book, *The Catcher in the Rye*. I looked up the meaning of every word I did not know in my little dictionary. I enjoyed the novel's teenage protagonist immensely, but the crying soul within me seemed never to cease.

My life before had been more about discipline, but now in Phanat Nikhom I started to lose it. At times I enjoyed drinking with the boys. Drinking, however, was only a temporary relief; it suppressed the crying soul by drowning it with alcohol, but every time I got up there was a severe headache and the scary emptiness within.

It seemed nothing could ease the emotional pain and the spiritual void I felt. Not even poetry helped. If someone said that poetry is the meaning of life, I would say to them it is not. I tried it, composing hundreds of poems with the hope of relief, to no avail. Poetry can only be a vehicle that leads us to the truth.

The more I saw the effects of torture on Dung, the more it made me think about Minh and Thanh and their deaths. It was painful to ask, "Why are they not here?" They intentionally escaped from Vietnam and from the army in search of a better life, yet the Khmer Rouge killed them both. I had not intended to escape in search of freedom, yet after years in captivity I was here in this camp enjoying freedom (even if only to a limited extent). I had lived while they had perished. Why?

The questions kept ringing in my mind, and I concluded, "You should look for the meaning of life out of this terrible experience." It was a persistent voice within. I identified it as the same urging voice I heard when I was lost in the Cambodian jungle. I was stubborn, but this urging was even more stubborn. Eventually I gave up and decided to go and seek the truth.

Marxist-Leninist Communism definitely had no answer for me. I gave it the thumbs down because of my experience in Vietnam and the hard evidence of the Khmer Rouge genocide. I liked the theory of an ideal society. However, because of this blind ideology, more than one-third of Cambodia's population had perished, and here in the camp I lived among thousands of disillusioned Vietnamese people. If any single person had been responsible for this doctrine, millions in the lands of revolution could have sued for negligence and stupidity.

Similarly, Confucianism seemed to me to be merely another concept of the ideal society that had nothing to do with the spiritual urging within me. Neither could I see that science could provide answers for my raging soul. I assumed that only religion could help me.

Normally, Indo-Chinese people, and Vietnamese in particular, will profess, "I am a Buddhist," when asked about their religion. This is because we all have a leaning towards the traditions of Buddhism. "It is our religion," we can say to our friends. I was no exception, even though I had no idea what Buddhism truly was. Any adherence I had to it came from prejudice and was based entirely on my preconception that Buddhism was the religion of my ancestors. So in searching for the truth, I assumed that Buddhism was the answer. Jesus Christ and Christianity were still, in my perception, a religion of the West. Even though God's children in the International Red Cross and YWAM (Youth With A Mission) showed me kindness and extended their hands to rescue me, their goodness could not overcome my inherent bias. Thus I chose Buddhism because I felt more at home with it; it was more Asian than I was. In choosing it, I felt I would have a religion more acceptable to tradition than the religion of the West.

I befriended many Buddhists and attached myself to the activities of the camp's largest temple. One of the highest-ranking Buddhists in the camp was a monk called Reverend Thich (not his real name). I befriended him, visited him and, of course, inquired further about the facts of Buddhism. This inquiry was more than curiosity; it was part of my deep quest, my heart's cry for answers for my life.

Of the many questions that kept ringing in me, one of the most urgent was, "Why am I still alive while others were killed?" I pounced on Reverend Thich as someone I thought could give me an answer. "Why was I in the same prison, undergoing the same torture, even enduring more than others, yet they died and I lived? Why did I survive the imprisonment of the Khmer Rouge longer than anyone else?" The urge at the back of my mind kept demanding, *I have to find out the reason why I'm still alive.*

One day, when we were drinking tea together, I asked Reverend Thich my burning question: "Why do I still live while others are dead?" He said many things in answer, but they boiled down to one main point: "Your *karma* has not ended!"

Karma, the belief that what we do in one life determines our fate, good or bad, in future reincarnations, is Hinduism and Buddhism in a nutshell. If there was truth in it, however, then I had extreme difficulty with the problem of the Khmer Rouge's killing fields. I politely raised my objection.

"It cannot be right that one-third of Cambodians, mostly intellectuals and the middle class, who lived good lives and were very Buddhist in their standards, were sent to such horrific deaths. Was that because of their *karma*? Can all their *karma* account for such a focused calamity at only one point in Cambodian history?"

I could not consider it acceptable to think that most Cambodian males, who had undergone three years of training in monasteries like monks, practicing alms and austerity in the temples, could be so easily dismissed as the *karma* theory suggested. If it was their bad old lives catching up with them, then where had all this concentrated evil come from?

Reverend Thich smiled and agreed that my questions were hard to answer.

In searching for the truth I was honest in my enquiries to Reverend Thich. He was presumably a nice man; he came from Da Nang in South Central Vietnam, yet he did not have any of the post-war agenda or hatred that many other South Vietnamese displayed towards those of us from the North. Our discussions were a mutual exchange of ideas in my spiritual search.

My quest for the truth in Buddhism ended suddenly, however, when a young nun accused Reverend Thich of harassment and sexual abuse. As an interpreter for the social work office, I had access to details of the case. I could not believe that such things could happen within the walls of a temple. As a person searching for the truth with the Reverend, I had to distance myself so I would not be accused of bias in his favor. I had to be fair in my translating for both accuser and plaintiff. Mountains of documents were provided by each side, the young nun and her supporters and Reverend Thich and his friends. All the writing was in Vietnamese and I had to translate it for the UNHCR and the social workers so they could understand the issues.

The case was brought to the Camp Commander, a Thai, who decided to put the accusation to a fair trial. In this trial he summoned both parties to a public hall in the middle of the camp so that everybody could see the proceedings and come to know the truth. That afternoon was the hardest day of my interpreting career. The monk never intended to answer the Camp Commander's questions; instead he kept procrastinating. Sometimes I did not even know what I was translating. He even used his position to challenge the Camp Commander when he pressed, "Does Thailand and its laws allow me to practice my religion of Buddhism?" Even more bizarrely, he accused the Camp Commander of belittling the old South Vietnamese yellow-and-red flag by flying it lower than the Thai national flag. It was an attempt to politicize the trial and divert attention from the accusation against him.

This was one of the strangest cases I had ever met and I was at a loss as to how to handle it. Perhaps my English was too limited because sometimes the people I was translating for pulled faces in puzzlement. I could see that Reverend Thich was trying to stir up a riot in the camp. Thank goodness people were sensible enough not to cause trouble.

The upshot of the trial was that the young nun was removed from the camp and Reverend Thich was discharged from the temple (though many Vietnamese still blindly supported him and he continued to live there). From that afternoon on, however, I realized that even this monk, whom I viewed as my friend, did not have high moral standards or any sense of ethical accountability. He had neither principles nor courage to face reality. So I decided he had no right to influence me or give me counsel. I could also see that he truly had nothing to offer me in my search for truth.

Thanks to Reverend Thich, my hope of finding answers in the religion of my forefathers came to an end. Nonetheless, my urge to search for meaning became more ardent. I started to go to the many religious meeting places in the camp. One was the Catholic Church, which was popular with many people because Catholicism is strong in Vietnam. Most Catholics from South Vietnam disliked the Communist regime so they left Vietnam in their thousands. Many of them welcomed me to their church, but somehow I found the bonding was too superficial and could not venture any further.

There were also branches of Buddhist sects such as Hòa Hảo and Cao Đài, and evangelical Christian and Seventh Day Adventist churches as well. I helped some of these groups from time to time when they were in need, but in terms of my search for truth, none of them interested me. My heart towards religion became increasingly cold. As a young boy, all that the Communists taught me in school about religion and the clerical class was that they were 'parasites on society'. If before I was sarcastic and distrustful of religion, now I became even more so.

One thing I noticed was that many groups seemed to favor their own members in giving aid to those in need in the camp. The Buddhists from Taiwan only helped those of Chinese ethnicity; the Vietnamese Buddhists only helped those who were Buddhists. There were times when Catholics and Buddhists who had settled in third countries sent money back to support the poor and those who had no relatives overseas. The motive was a good heart to help the people of the camp who were in need, but as usual the aid never reached us, the captured soldiers. I personally didn't need it; I had been self-sufficient for more than 20 years. The UN's provision was enough for me, and I could work to make ends meet. But if people were kind enough to send money to give out to the destitute, then Dung and a few others in our group were good candidates. Those distributing aid were not supposed to treat us differently. It was like spitting in our faces.

It was hard to seek the truth from those who were so indifferent in their souls. As soon as these religious people heard my accent, I saw the expression on their faces change.

Well, if there was nothing to seek from them, then perhaps

tobacco and alcohol could help ease the pain within. Although we did not have much money, I and a few others worked in the camp shops, so we pooled our resources and bought alcohol from the Thai soldiers outside the barbed wired fence. Cannabis and other hard drugs were available, but I never touched them because I had seen their effect on young soldiers in Cambodia. Alcohol was my choice.

When I drank, then of course Dung and a few others also joined in. We 'drank to forget'—that was our motivation. It eased our minds and also helped us in our quest for sleep. Sometimes when we drank we would sing, not patriotic songs anymore, but defiant songs like *Chúng ta là những kẻ; ma chê, quỷ trách, ông vải hờn, phái đoàn khinh:*

We are the ones that ghosts fear,
the devil avoids,
our ancestors fail to recognize,
and the delegations ignore and reject.

Seeing no future also helped the daredevils among us become even more adventurous. We trapped dogs belonging to Thais outside the camp. We also bought dogs as meat from the poor soldiers who didn't mind catching them or shooting them for us. A live dog cost us 30 baht, a dead one with a bullet hole, 20 baht. The Thai soldiers and guards enjoyed doing business with us.

We even laid bets with each other to trap security dogs for meat. All dogs are the same, but dog meat from security and army dogs was worth more. It was an evil game. We ex-soldiers liked to take risks, so the higher the rank of the officers whose dogs we stole, the higher our winnings. Of course it was dangerous, and we faced imprisonment or even death if the Thai security personnel discovered that we were the main culprits behind their missing animals. Therefore, whenever we caught dogs from security personnel or soldiers, we had to limit those we invited to our parties. Loose-lipped people never got invited to share our prize. The security personnel knew that people in the camp trapped their dogs for meat, but they could find no evidence to charge anyone.

I had now reached the point where I was busier trying to catch dogs from the Thais outside the camp than studying. I and my friends had lost much of our interest in living with care.

I also began to fall in love with girls. Often my friends and I blinded ourselves and thought what we were experiencing was love, but it was not—it was lust to satisfy the body. This, like all my other attempts to quell the inner urge, was just bandaging the bleeding wound. My past had not been dealt with, and I had no idea how to deal with it. The girls in Phanat Nikhom had the same issues. They had left home by themselves, they were lonely and lost, and they saw us as rogue guys who might be able to protect them from other predators. So they offered themselves. Many of the ex-soldiers took advantage of this and I became a bit jealous of them.

Of course, I finally fell in love with a girl. A beautiful young lady came to the camp as a refugee with her family and became a volunteer worker with us at the American Refugee Committee. She was the first woman in the world who made my heart melt with love. But I was young, naive, arrogant and clumsy with her, so one day out of frustration she wrote a letter in red ink to tell me to back off: "You will never be allowed to come to see me or anyone in my family—you freak!" She forbade me to ever see her or talk to her again.

I took her words to heart and was silly enough not to approach her to apologize, or at least to probe to see what the problem was. "I have not begged for life and I will not beg for love," I stupidly told myself. My stubbornness only increased the pain in my heart. Had I learnt to be humble before her, then I could have saved all the hurt. My brokenness and foolishness had destroyed love, damaged the one I loved and damaged myself even further. I was learning that falling in love is easy, but keeping love healthy is another matter.

I was carrying a deep inner wound, so it is no wonder love was so superficial for me. Just as a broken vessel cannot hold water, so I could not hold genuine love for long. The wounded heart, the bruised soul and the undiscovered truth cannot bring out the best from love. This generated more pain, suffering and frustration. My soul became seared and hardened until I felt almost nothing. I tried to love as genuinely as I could, but my inner being was too broken.

I did not know what to do with this part of myself. My heart ached and my head ached, but I stubbornly refused to allow God to carry my burden. I only overcame this inner wretchedness when I later allowed God to perform His master touch in my soul, which transformed me to wholeness and a brand new life.

During those painful days, one positive aspect was that I took up keeping a diary and composing poems. This was the most productive literary period of my life. I wrote numerous love poems and poems of heartbreak—today these are my only treasure from my years at Phanat Nikhom. Later on I fell in love again with another girl, a merchant's only daughter from Ho Chi Minh City. We met when she helped me during a time of sickness. She had a large family in America that had small businesses in Washington and LA. It was a short but painful relationship. Lan resettled in America in 1988 before I was accepted to resettle in Australia. We promised each other we would marry, but it was a false promise. It hurt us both deeply.

Since Phanat Nikhom was essentially a transit center where people lived while waiting for resettlement, most relationships were temporary. My inability to maintain a good, solid relationship frustrated me intensely, but most men didn't feel that way. They were just happy to have fun.

Han, my youngest housemate, asked one day, "Because girls come to visit us, why don't we make our home more presentable? What we need is some wallpaper to make it a bit nicer."

Everyone agreed. Thanh, a Catholic, suggested, "Other people have money to buy wallpaper from the market outside the camp. We also have money. Why can't we——"

He had no chance to finish his sentence before he was stopped by the others. "That's no good. All our money should be saved for cigarettes, alcohol, and parties." We had to find other means.

A few days later I was passing the Seventh Day Adventist Church and noticed a pile of free Vietnamese Bibles on a table. That gave me a bright idea.

I shared it with the boys: "The Seventh Day Adventist Church is giving out free Vietnamese Bibles. I'll go and ask the man for a Bible, and then we can rip it up to make the wallpaper." I paused to see how they would react. "What do you guys think?"

It was thumbs up from all of them. "Why waste money on wallpaper when we can use that book for it?" they all laughed, even Thanh the Catholic. They seemed to think the idea was brilliant.

The next day I went to the Seventh Day Adventists, pretending to be interested in religion, and approached Ngoc, the man in charge of the local church. "Can I have two Bibles for the boys to read?" I asked him with false humility. I knew I would get them anyway; if I couldn't have them by asking, I would come and steal them at night.

Ngoc was a good man but a bit naïve. After hearing that a guy like me wanted two Bibles, without a thought he ran to his office, took two new Gideon Bibles, and gave them to me.

"Let me sign my name for you!" Ngoc signed his name under the black cover.

As I took the two Bibles home, I laughed as if they were trophies. The boys got excited about them as well. I told them about Ngoc, imitating his voice and the way he signed the Bibles for me. We had a good chuckle.

The next day we took apart the Bibles page by page. We used most of the pages as wallpaper and the rest for cigarettes. Four of us worked on sticking the pages to the walls. But none of us was interested in reading them in depth. While we worked we made fun of the Bible and all religions, monks and priests; it seemed no one escaped our foul jokes that day. Han in particular enjoyed ripping the pages out and reading a few words to make us laugh.

Oh, how sinful, how arrogant we were! And I was the chief architect of this act. I have deeply repented of it since. Had God not shown up later in my life, I would be forever condemned.

But God had His own way of getting my attention. And this time He got things His way, not my way. We ripped up the pages of the Bible and sang funny songs, but in the heart of God, even though He felt the pain of the ignorance of our youth, I think He was saying to Himself, "I will get you, and you will suffer with me."

Chapter eighteen

AT NOON IN THE REFUGEE CAMP

Imprisonment and torture with the Khmer Rouge had taught me a lesson about humility. There I learnt that God in heaven was the supreme authority in nature. But knowing that was different from knowing Jesus as Savior and personal friend. In that sense I was truly not a humble man. People can talk about God in all manner of ways to justify their religious piety, yet like myself still have no idea of what the ultimate value of humility is and how to be a friend of God.

It was one noon time in the hot summer of Thailand. We often joked that, "in Thailand there is only hot and hotter." When the weather was hot in the refugee camp we had nothing to do, so we enjoyed a midday siesta. But that day it was so hot I could not sleep. Tossing and turning on my bed, I rolled to face the wall—and there in front of me was our strange wallpaper. Somehow the pages had been pasted up in order, and right before my eyes the entire eleventh chapter of Ecclesiastes was spread out. I read these extraordinary words:

Have joy, O young man, while you are young; and let your heart be glad in the days of your strength, and go in the ways of your heart, and in the desire of your eyes; but be certain that for all these things God will be your judge. (Ecclesiastes 11:9)

The Spirit of the Lord made me pay attention to these words of the wise. This warning began to sink into my heart. The words were simple, yet they had an ominous meaning. As a young man I could enjoy doing whatever I wished, but the Lord God was right here, and He would judge. He would punish my evilness.

Imprisonment by both the Khmer Rouge and the Thais had taught me to fear punishment. With humans I could lie, but with the Supreme God I had nowhere to hide. I could not run away from all my rotten behavior and evil thoughts.

I stopped reading and lay there, sweating, looking at the low ceiling. One thought gripped my mind: *I will be judged.* The Supreme God I had prayed to in the jungle would one day ask me what I had done with my life, and I could not find any good and logical answer for Him. I felt the pain of my ignorance and arrogance. I had no excuse.

I turned back to the wall. The Bible was right there, laid out for me to read. One page, then the next, and the next—all collated and glued to the wall.

"What is this?" I asked myself. "How come these words are so real and alive to me?"

I wondered why Ngoc had given me the Bible with no intention of explaining it to me. Perhaps, even if he had tried to, I would not have understood, and whatever passage he chose would not have had any effect. It must have been the work of the Spirit of God to allow us to tear the Bible up and stick it right beside my bed so that I could not avoid it.

I began to enjoy reading my wallpaper Bible. I finished several chapters in Proverbs and a few Psalms because they were in the same area of wallpaper. I had to sit up to read more. That noon time reading piqued my curiosity about the Bible and its contents. Sure, the pages were stuck to my bedroom wall, and they were not complete because other pages were plastered to surrounding walls or we had already 'smoked' them. But that afternoon my hardened heart began melting. The right verse at the right time from the right angle touched me and brought about the fear of God. I suddenly had a desire to own a Bible and this time not rip it apart, but to cherish it and think over its messages and contents.

I was like a treasure hunter who had found on a map where to find his prize—or like myself in the dry jungle, finding life-saving water.

Over the following months my wall became a reading board for me until one day heavy rain soaked the house and destroyed the wallpaper. I regretted that I could not continue with my reading. I wanted to know how the book went on. I wanted to understand more. But I was too shy, too ashamed, too fearful and even too guilty to go to the church and ask for another Bible.

Had I humbled myself then, salvation may have come to my soul earlier than it did and saved me from more heartaches and headaches on my journey. Yet I still give the credit to the Holy Spirit, who alone led me to Jesus Christ. Perhaps the Lord allowed it to happen the way it did so I could digest what I had read and look more deeply into my soul until the day I was desperate enough and until there was a church available to me that would nurture and strengthen my commitment to Him.

By this time I had been rejected by delegations from two countries. The hurt of rejection was still fresh and the prospect of future resettlement in another country was dim. I had not found any hope yet. But just as when I was dying of thirst in the jungle, I now had a need. "Why should I stay any longer in this refugee camp?" I asked myself. "Why shouldn't I ask the heavenly Lord again to intervene with my resettlement?" I needed a miracle for my future just as much as I had when standing in the dry jungle streambed years before.

Since the day I first arrived at Phanat Nikhom, the people from YWAM had attracted me, but my preconceived ideas about Eastern and Western religions had prevented me from getting closer to them. YWAM was a Christian organization that was truly helping us, but though I could see their good actions, I was too blind to see what drove them to do them. I had no chance to work with them, but from a distance, as a soldier trained to observe, I saw their work and their lifestyle. They were neat, punctual, effective, disciplined and fun-loving, all of which made them even more attractive. The serenity in their faces and the ethics of their work made me see they were different.

I knew they were believers in God, but for a long time I refused to ask them about their faith. Yet they had something that others didn't have. I asked myself, "Why *not* go and ask them? Find out what makes these young men and women come to work in a refugee camp, and what their reasons are for having such confidence and joy."

I began to think: *Well, this Western religion obviously produces good people. If it's the Bible that tells them about wisdom and God, then why shouldn't I give it a try? Maybe this time my luck will be better.* My old urge to seek truth was reasserting itself.

One day I took courage and went to two ladies from YWAM; they were from Scandinavia. I asked a very odd question.

"Would you please tell me—why did you come to this camp to work and help us while our own people are too busy fighting each other?"

One of the ladies looked very ordinary, but she had a very cheerful heart. A broad smile showed on her face as she answered, "Because we have been blessed so much that we wanted to come here and share with you guys a few of the blessings."

Her answer came automatically, innocently, without any deep thinking or trace of pretention. No one expects someone to come and ask a question like that, so her response was spontaneous. She had no intention to impress me with deep philosophical ideas. She simply said she meant to share her life and the blessing she had received with us, the refugee people. The word 'blessing' intrigued me most.

I did not continue the conversation because I had only enough courage to ask one question, and that was it. But her answer was enough for me to go home and ponder.

In life I had been through so much and had received so much blessing, but I had not yet experienced blessing from the Lord's point of view. I was still focused on the issue of resettlement, and it seemed my time in Phanat Nikhom would go on forever. We ex-soldiers were traumatized again when two of our group, Toi and Nghiep, could not contain their frustration any longer. They soaked themselves with petrol and set fire to themselves. Nghiep was rescued in time, but Toi was not. He was later confirmed dead. As well, more men began to leave the camp to follow the bloodthirsty warmongers in the dream of recapturing Vietnam. But what could I do? I had no choice but to remain.

'Blessing,' the word the Scandinavian lady used, reminded

me of our wish, our drive for better behavior. Yes, I wanted the blessings she had. I still naively shied away from the source of all blessing, God Himself; but He knew that one day I would be in His arms and would journey alongside Him.

By now I was desperate to be accepted by a foreign delegation for resettlement. Any country would do. I had been living in Phanat Nikhom for four long years. It was enough. I truly, sincerely desired to live a normal life. Again the thought came to me that I needed the intervention of the Supreme Authority over my resettlement. What He had done for me in the Cambodian jungle, He could do for me in my present situation.

I made a quiet prayer to the unknown God, just as I had prayed in the jungle when I was lost. "Lord, if I am accepted by a delegation in the next few months, then I will worship you."

I was naïve. What right did I have to set the Creator God conditions? Who was I to tell Him what to do? I should obey Him, not ask Him to appease me, a little arrogant creature. But this attitude is usual for people from other faiths; they think they can make their gods be their servants. I had not yet learned that the Lord of Heaven is not a genie who is there to fulfill my wish list. But God is a God of grace and does as He pleases. He knows how silly His children are, yet He still carries them on His wings and carries out their wishes, like the father for his prodigal son in Jesus' parable, to get their attention.

Two months later an Australian delegation came and I was called to an interview. To my amazement, the interviewer, a man named Bob, looked through my résumés and saw evidence of a hard-working person. He seemed to like my honesty when I dared to tell him, as I had told Paul from the Canadian delegation, that I was born in North Vietnam and was an ex-soldier. Bob smiled and said, "I don't care much about that. It's what you will do in the future that counts, not your past."

The interview with the Australian delegation was the shortest and sweetest. I admired Bob's Aussie straightforwardness and dry sense of humor. I vowed to myself that day that I would be a blessing to his nation, not a burden—part of the solution, not a problem. That day, I went home and began to feel joy in my heart.

I had a future.

The word of 'blessing' began to ring true. Of course, I told the people in YWAM that I had been accepted by the Australian delegation and would be leaving the camp soon. They celebrated with me.

Chapter nineteen

TO AUSTRALIA

Soon after my interview I received a letter, via the UNHCR, from the Australian Embassy in Bangkok. It stated: "You have been accepted by the Australian delegation for the humanitarian program and should prepare for departure soon." I had expected the news, yet it still brought me a feeling of total excitement for the entire day. Only someone who has been in my shoes could understand my feelings.

More than seven long years had passed since I left home in Vietnam. Six years of imprisonment and confinement had stolen most of that time. I held the letter of acceptance from the Australians in my hand, overjoyed. Knowing that I would be leaving Phanat Nikhom very soon made my heart jump and my soul dance. It released my deep frustration to know I would soon be free to embrace the opportunity to live a normal life again.

I stood in the office of the social worker, Khun Saroj, and kept a few minutes of silence, pouring out my thankful heart to the One who had opened this door for me—and of course to the government and people of Australia.

Khun Saroj smiled at me. "You should be very happy today," she said, her soft voice cutting through my quiet moment.

I broke into a broad smile. "Yes, mother—I am over the moon!"

Khun Saroj was in her seventies, and many of us in Phanat Nikhom, especially the ex-soldiers, called her 'mother' because of the motherly care she gave to all. To be a social worker in a refugee camp, where the majority of residents were in grief from loss, pain, ignorance, and suffering, must have been hard, yet Khun Saroj always remained dignified. She gave me a look that deeply shared my joy.

"Do you know when you will go to Australia?" she asked in the caring tone of voice that is famously Thai.

"Not yet. I only received this letter today. But I hope it will be soon. The sooner the better."

Indeed, I dreamed that my life would be much better in Australia than in this camp, much better than in the Cambodian jungle and the Khmer Rouge prison and much better than in Vietnam, where I had experienced so much pain from early childhood. I was truly excited about the prospect of boarding a bus to be ferried to the land of Australia. Although I had no idea of the country or its people, if they were kind and generous enough to accept me, I would go there with joy.

Knowing Khun Saroj had a Catholic background, I shared more details with her. "The Australian Embassy also informed me that they have found a group of Catholic Christians who are willing to sponsor and support me to live in Sydney. They gave the address of the group, and I will waste no time in writing a thank you letter to each of them." I hurried home to do just that.

The waiting time passed, though not fast enough. All candidates for Australia had to undergo the Australian Orientation Program prior to departure. We learnt a bit about Australian culture from video clips, and then on 17 April, 1989, I left Phanat Nikhom and headed to Australia.

Early that morning, Dung and a few other friends accompanied me to the gate of the camp. My emotions were very mixed when I said goodbye. I had never felt like it before. On the one hand, I was excited and anxious about my future in the new country I knew so little about, with its promise of freedom and a better life. On the other hand, I was deeply concerned for my friends, especially Dung. I had lived with him for five years and we had been through so much together. I had been his friend, his confidant and his defender from abuse. "If anyone touches Dung that means they touch me," I solemnly told people, and they knew I meant it. Dung had lived with me and found solid support, so the attachment between us had grown very strong. But now I was leaving him behind, and I couldn't be sure of anything regarding his future. If he had had a sound mind like the others, I would have been less concerned, but with his mental state he was very vulnerable.

The time came to leave. Emotion ran high as I stepped onto the bus. In my old fashion, I still tried to conceal my feelings and waved goodbye to everybody. The bus slowly headed to the airport.

Whispering to myself, I said, "Goodbye, camp. Goodbye, Dung. Goodbye, friends. I can't promise you anything, Dung, but when I reach my new country, I will see if I can sponsor you to come and join me." It was a silent vow; since I had failed to keep my promise to my mother, I refused to promise anything to anybody if it was beyond my capacity.

I did try to fulfill my vow. I introduced Dung to the group of Christians who sponsored me, and they did their best to bring him to Sydney. But by the time the sponsorship was processed, Dung had been interviewed by a Canadian delegation, which kindly opened the door for him to that nation. He departed for Canada, and I lost touch with him.

I may have left Thailand and the refugee camp, even Cambodia and Vietnam, but the wars, the betrayal, the physical and emotional wounding, and the trauma had only just begun to surface. I was in a new country but my heart was old and scarred.

My excitement about my new life in Australia only lasted for a little while. My old bad habits were still there and followed me wherever I went. Like the crippled woman doubled up with pain in the Gospels (Luke 13:10–13), I could only be healed by the mighty touch of the Lord Jesus Christ. Her healing did not come by her own effort, and my healing would not come by mine.

When I arrived at Sydney International Airport, the group of faithful Catholic people who had sponsored me was waiting to welcome me. Knowing I was lonely, they visited me often at Westbridge Migrant Hostel in Villawood, Western Sydney (now an Immigration Detention Centre).

"You can stay here for a little while to finish all the paperwork, then we will organize for you to live in another, better place," two of the sponsors, Jenny and a nun named Gloria, told me. They kept their word, and after less than two weeks in the hostel, they kindly took me to live in Crows Nest on Sydney's North Shore. There I shared a house with a few other disadvantaged young men, several of them Vietnamese.

It was the first time I had ever been exposed to a sophisticated lifestyle like that of the North Shore. I was born on a collective farm, grew up in the midst of war and went into the jungle trained to fight. I had endured great deprivation and want in prison and the refugee camp. I had never experienced affluence in my entire life. All the good things in this new society scared me to death, and I was totally out of my depth. I became extremely lonely and depressed. It was a rapid change and I could not cope. In farming, schooling, the army, prison and the refugee camp, my life over there may have been disparaging and despairing, but at least it was truly laid back! Now in North Shore society, which was so highly organized and time efficient, I felt lost.

I had always been busy before, always ready to bury my life in work and study. If there was any free time then I drank and partied with friends until we passed out. Now I knew no one as a close friend—no one I could talk with freely—and of course I did not have money or confidence to go out to buy a drink. So I began to feel disillusioned. Night after night I had to fight hard to get myself to sleep. And sleep was now something I was wishing for. Adapting to this new individualistic lifestyle was a tough challenge for me.

I must hasten to say that this was through no fault of my sponsors. I can't describe how much I owe to them: Jenny (whom I came to call 'Mum'), Greg and his wife Eloise, and Gloria. Without their support I would never have come to Australia. Without their help in the first few weeks here, I would not have known what to do with myself. I can never repay them for what they did. I continue to pray that the Lord will bless them and increase their kindness to all people.

During the time I stayed in the halfway house in Crows Nest, they came to visit me often despite holding down full-time jobs. Greg and Eloise took me everywhere—they helped me register my name for social security, open a bank account, sign up for an English course and gain job-seeking skills. All of these aspects of Australian life were truly alien to me, and without their help I would have been as lost as I was in the Cambodian jungle.

Through Jenny and Gloria I also came to know two young men, David and Jonathan. Even though they were very busy with their daily routine, they came to the house and gave me free English tutoring. Because my English was self-taught, there were plenty of grammatical mistakes for them to fix up.

One Friday night, Jonathan, a lawyer, came to our home with his face ablaze with excitement. "We've just come from a meeting with Dr. Haing Ngor in Darling Harbor," he said. "He's such an inspiring movie star!" Jonathan talked excitedly about shaking hands with the famous actor and showed us Ngor's signature. In my ignorance, I had no idea who he was. I didn't know he was the main actor in a famous film about the Khmer Rouge, *The Killing Fields*.

At that time I had not seen the movie so I could not appreciate Ngor and his efforts to depict the situation in Cambodia in 'Year Zero', when Pol Pot took over (1975). Later, when I actually saw the film, I realized my knowledge of the Khmer Rouge went far beyond what was depicted on the screen. The movie was only the tip of the iceberg. It cost me a lot of sweat and tears to watch it, and I felt sick throughout. However, I was very appreciative of Ngor's attempt to portray through the camera lens a portion of Cambodia's suffering.

When Jonathan spoke so enthusiastically about the film that Friday night, I thought to myself, *The real thing is here in front of you but you have not seen it yet.* My mind, however, told me to keep silent and reveal nothing about my own story. I was in a new country; I didn't know the people, so I could not trust anyone or tell them about my past life. In some ways, people enjoy an actor playing a role more than the reality of life. I was not an actor; I was a real person. But I had no strength to confide in anybody. (Only when I became a believer in Christ Jesus and was convinced that a good Christian community would help me did I open up.)

I lived in Crows Nest for about ten weeks, and during that period I returned to Westbridge three times in the hope of finding any friends from the refugee camp who may have arrived in

Sydney. It was the habit of an old soldier trained to go back to look for those lost in action. I was well known in the camp, and all I needed to do was stand near the kitchen gate and watch for anybody I recognized.

One day, however, I was unable to wait for dinner time, so I went to the office of the hostel social worker, Mrs Lieu. I asked her about any newcomers from Thailand. She was not allowed to give me any information because there had been incidents of previously resettled refugees coming back to the hostel to abuse others or settle old scores from the camp with violence. But then her eyes suddenly sparked.

"Your name is Uong, isn't it?" she said. She looked at me through her thick glasses. "A person came here looking for you last week."

I thought it must be a mistake. I had no friends in Australia; all my friends had gone to France or Scandinavia.

"Who was it?" I asked. "A man or woman?"

"She was a young lady of Caucasian appearance," Lieu replied. That surprised me even more because I had no friends of Caucasian appearance. Lieu nevertheless gave me the woman's telephone number. "She told me that if you ever came back here, you could contact her." The name beside the number was *Lyn Daniel*.

Back home in Crows Nest that night, I rang the number looking for the mystery woman. We had little time to talk, but I did ask my two most pressing questions: "How do you know my name, and how did you know I was in Australia?"

Lyn spoke very clear English and intentionally slowed down so I could understand her. It made a good first impression.

"I know Marion, your friend from YWAM in Phanat Nikhom refugee camp," she explained. "She wrote to me and asked me to look out for you. Do you remember her? When I received her letter I came to visit you in the hostel, but you'd already left." She asked for my address and promised to visit me the following Wednesday.

I remembered Marion. She had given me a Good News Bible just before I left Phanat Nikhom for Australia. I mused: *So this lady, Lyn Daniel, is connected with YWAM. She must be a good person.*

On Wednesday afternoon I was ready and waiting for her to come. I even went out to the road to welcome her.

"Do you drink coffee?" I asked as a courtesy.

She looked at me and my housemates with unusual big eyes and nodded, "Yes, thanks."

It was the first time I had ever made coffee. I had no idea what to do. I remembered how the men in the refugee camp made Vietnamese coffee with condensed milk, so I followed suit. It took me almost half an hour to pour an entire can of condensed milk into two large cups, one for her and one for me. Each had about two spoonfuls of coffee. Then I poured hot water on top. The condensed milk had been stored in the refrigerator for a while and had thickened. As it almost filled the cup, by the time I gave her the coffee, the spoon was standing upright in the middle of the thick liquid.

She gave me a strange look, and a few of the boys from the house also looked at me bizarrely. I knew I must have done something wrong, but I just had to ignore them. Only later, after Lyn left, did the boys enlighten me. "How can it take you so long to make a cup of coffee? Why did you pour so much condensed milk into her cup? And why so much coffee?"

They called me *Ông ngố* (Mr Fool) and had a hearty laugh at my expense. I realized how silly I had been and regretted it deeply. Poor Lyn, she couldn't finish the whole cup of coffee that evening, and I bet she couldn't sleep much because of the strong dose. Despite this unpromising beginning, however, from that first meeting we became friends.

During my time in Crows Nest, I went with Jenny to many Catholic churches for Mass. I also made my first visit to a Catholic cathedral. Even though these visits were in the evening, the magnificent way the Catholics designed their buildings and the way they carried out the Mass was an awesome experience for me. When I moved from the halfway house to a granny flat behind Jenny's home in Eastwood, I continued to go to Mass whenever she was available to take me. Nevertheless, despite months of going to church, I never had a chance to talk to anybody personally, apart from Jenny. Everyone rushed home after the service. Nobody greeted me; nobody explained anything about the Catholic Church or the rituals of the Mass. No one even gave me an affectionate handshake. The community had done a great work for me personally, and I am forever in debt to them. But at the same time, this community of great works had lost its voice and the ability to explain itself to a searching and crying heart.

There were times during these services when I sat feeling at odds with the crowd, lowering my eyes because I had no idea what was going on. I merely imitated what Jenny and the rest of the people did. As an adult and an ex-soldier with a reasonable mind, when I did not know what I was doing I felt bored and tired. These acts of imitation were irrelevant, and worse, they made me feel stupid. However, I was patient and willing to go with Jenny, or anybody else who would take me, because my heart was indeed looking for answers to the questions that had bugged me for so long.

Chapter twenty

BECOMING A CHILD OF GOD

But where sin increased, grace increased all the more.
(Romans 5:20)

Thanks to Lyn Daniel, my quest for answers was about to take a new direction. She introduced me to her own church, a small group of charismatic Christians in Cabramatta.

In the middle of 1989, the church (now known as Jesus Family Centre) had fewer than a dozen people, including me. It was a new fellowship being planted by Lyn's home church in New Zealand. (Lyn was a New Zealander). The believers met in the living room of a three-bedroom house. I soon started attending every Sunday morning. It took me about 30 minutes to walk from my home to Eastwood train station, then an hour or more to Cabramatta in southwest Sydney. I missed the train many times and often got lost at other stations. But it did not deter me from going. Sunday was indeed my day for searching for truth.

I went to the church often but did not understand the preaching. I had to work hard to translate the message from English to Vietnamese in my head. At the same time, because I was having problems sleeping—as I'd had since arriving in Australia—I frequently fell asleep during the service. It took about ten minutes of preaching and then I was gone, deep asleep on the couch. I don't know what the young pastor felt when there were only a dozen people in the room and one young man in the front row always slept and even snored. Thank God for the grace that He gave those people and the extraordinary acceptance they showed me. I never heard a rebuke from them, and no one ever asked, "Why are you always asleep in the service?" Despite my bizarre behavior, the group demonstrated their Christ-like life to me, and that summed up their way of discipleship in a nutshell.

Another thing that touched me was that I could easily identify with this group of Christians, and I found them willing to listen and very easy to talk to. They were easy to laugh with and communicated with each other freely, and on a very personal level. The group had a family-like atmosphere. After the service we always sat down and had a meal together. Meal times became very important in my life and still are today. I had not experienced a family atmosphere for a long time and had missed it dearly. In this very small gathering, suddenly I found I had a family like mine in Vietnam. Here we could eat, talk, and share, and it reminded me of my own family with my father at the head and children running around having fun.

Despite my lack of understanding and tendency to fall asleep, I did notice one thing after a few visits: they talked often about a person named Jesus Christ and salvation in Him. I began to think I needed to identify with this group of Christians. I felt I was 'ready' for their God.

On Sunday 9 August, 1989, I had my opportunity. At the end of the service the pastor said, "If there's anyone in the meeting today who wants to give their life to the Lord, stand up." It was a random invitation, but I still had the attitude of a soldier so I stood up without hesitation. It shocked the young preacher—I don't think he was prepared for my response.

I stood there all by myself among the dozen believers, waiting to see what this 'priest' was going to do with me. (At that time I had no idea of the distinction between a pastor and a priest. They all seemed the same to me.)

The pastor looked me in the eye. "So, do you want to accept the Lord Jesus into your life today?" he asked.

I had no real understanding of the question, but I replied, "Yes, I do!"

"Then raise your hands and repeat these words after me."

I still had no idea what I was really doing, but I raised no objection. He led me to pray a sinner's prayer and after that confirmed, "You have accepted the Lord Jesus as your personal Savior and friend today. Now you are my brother."

That brought me up sharply. I had accepted Jesus as my Lord and Savior that day, but the term 'brother' was hard for me to grasp. He was white and I was brown, so how could we become brothers in just that moment? Was life that easy?

The group looked ecstatic, and they were even happier after the service and during lunch. I kept asking myself, "Why are all these people so happy today?" I dared not ask because of fear they might think I was stupid or too curious. I assumed they were just happy and didn't mind being happy with them.

Nowadays, as a pastor myself, I understand why they were so happy.

I say to you that even so there will be more joy in heaven when one sinner is turned away from his wrongdoing, than for ninety-nine good men, who have no need of a change of heart. . . . There is joy among the angels of God, when one sinner is turned away from his wrongdoing. (Luke 15:7, 10 BBE)

Every time I lead a person to accept the Lord Jesus as his or her personal Savior, my emotions run very high because heaven rejoices for every soul that comes back to the Lord.

Salvation had come to me that day, but to work out the value of that salvation and to tremble at it took me many months. This was the trail that the Lord allowed me to travel on my journey towards Him. I learnt the hard lesson of struggling to remain true to the faith, and of course I underwent a lot of ups and downs with much sweat and many misunderstandings. As a new child of God I needed time to digest His food, and I needed His grace so that I could grow to maturity.

While I was living in the half-way house, I began a course called 'English for Further Study' at North Sydney Institute of TAFE in Gore Hill. I wanted to further my education and enter Macquarie University so I could be trained in journalism, a career I admired and loved. At home in Vietnam I had eyed such a course but was prevented from taking it by military conscription. I still wanted this to be my future career. However, once again things didn't work out; it took me another ten years to achieve my goal of studying journalism. But I now know this was the Lord redirecting my desire to work as a journalist and calling me to serve Him.

In November 1989 I received two devastating letters in one single day. The first was from Lan, my girlfriend from Phanat Nikhom, who had resettled in America. She wrote:

After much consideration, and subject to my family's intervention, I have decided that I will not come to be with you in Australia. That means our relationship also should be terminated. Since you went to Australia, it seems our differences have become irreconcilable, and I think it will be much better for both of us to stop this relationship. I know this letter will hurt you tremendously, but I would rather have a short time of pain than a whole life lived in tension and arguments. It will be sad for you, but do not drink too hard as you always did in the refugee camp. I am not coming, but you will still remain a friend in my heart.

It was devastating news for me because her decision was so sudden, so abrupt. All I dreamed about was to have a family in this new country and together rebuild our lives. Her letter was like a knife that cut through my heart. I loved her dearly, and I had promised myself that I would work hard to establish my own family. That dream evaporated in an instant. I never imagined that she would decide to terminate our relationship.

Shocked and numb, I felt the emotional hurt flooding my whole being. Failure to love and rejection can be quite devastating. It was more painful than any physical hurt I had undergone. I didn't know whether I was mature enough to take this knock and still be 'fine' with her.

The world was suddenly very dark. I threw myself onto the bed and allowed myself to cry from the pain of losing her and being let down by someone I had loved and treasured. I sweated and sweated hard; it was as though the malaria was attacking me again.

After a while I grew curious about the second letter. It was from Vietnam and I knew it was from my second sister. As I opened it, I saw it was rather short and to the point, with only a few lines. I realized my sister had written it in a hurry:

We took Mum to hospital yesterday, with various problems. She may even lose her eyesight from cataracts, and urgently needs a special operation. She may not come out of it okay.

After reading these two letters I felt like I had been punched in the face and the stomach at the same time. My beloved mother, whom I adored and respected and whom I had always wanted to repay for all her endurance and suffering, was now hospitalized! I plunged into a even deeper distress.

I had only contacted Mum in late 1988 after I received the acceptance letter from the Australian Embassy. During my years in the refugee camp I refused to contact home because I wanted the Vietnamese government to pay for my parents' well-being. I knew the government would inform my parents that their son had been lost in action and that in consequence they were entitled to social support. I could do nothing to help them from the camp. Moreover, if the government had found out I was alive and a refugee in Thailand, not only would my parents' social allowance be cut, but my two younger siblings would undergo ridicule and be banned from all future education and career opportunities.

Even though I missed my mother and father dearly, I eased the pain by pouring all my sentiment for them into poems and other writings, which I never sent. I had to endure the separation and let the government repay them.

Now in this new land I could help them out, but news like that in my sister's letter broke my heart. Nothing I could do would ease the pain. Lan had a mind of her own; she could survive without me. After all, she was the one who had terminated the relationship, and I knew I had kept my word to her and remained faithful while waiting for her. With Mum it was another story. She was old and lived far away. Her eyes had become weary, perhaps through years of hardship and tears. And I still owed her my promise to return.

I suddenly had a deep desire to go home, cook and serve her a few meals, wash her clothes, and do the acts of a filial son for his mother. She deserved all the best from me before she died, but it seemed she would not survive before I returned home, and she could not afford the treatment she needed without my help. I had utterly failed to realize both my desires—to marry my girlfriend and to see my mother. The world seemed to have fallen apart.

Besides this new pressure, my long-suffering past had not been dealt with, so this new pain was like compound interest in a bank. It multiplied. I could not cope anymore, and that night I became physically ill. I felt the chilly cold that signaled malaria was resurfacing again.

What could I do to forget all this misery? For the first time in my life I became frantic and volatile. In danger of death I could build up defense mechanisms, but in this new situation my defensive skills were inadequate. Love attacked from the inside out, and that was unbearable. Failing to keep my promise to Mum was an internal anguish. My strong will was being squeezed from all sides.

From Eastwood, I immediately contacted some old Vietnamese acquaintances from Phanat Nikhom who were living in Cabramatta and asked whether they had room for me to move down there to find a job. Sadly, I was culturally insensitive to Jenny, only informing her in the afternoon that I was about to leave the granny flat in her backyard I had rented. Everything I did at that moment was hasty. When I realized much later and apologized, she graciously said she had not been upset because she had known many refugees and understood our culture.

After I moved to Cabramatta, my old friends helped me to find a job quickly—in the early '90s jobs were plentiful. They also became my new drinking friends. "Birds of a feather flock together" is an appropriate saying.

With money in hand I could now help Mum. But the trouble was, when a person has money and his soul is troubled, life becomes like quicksand. Alcohol was readily available, so I drowned myself in it again, just like in the refugee camp. I was on the run—running away from life—but this time I was running towards alcoholism.

Every evening after work, I drowned myself with beer to put myself to sleep. At the weekend it was party time, and we drank hardcore alcohol—in the refugee camp we had used cheap wine, but now that we had money, we drank quality stuff. Every Friday evening we rang each other up and organized which house to meet at.

In Phanat Nikhom there was a curfew which we had to obey to prevent disorder, but now we had total freedom and could go all night. More money was poured down the sewer than anywhere else. All the expensive alcohol and food ended up being vomited into the toilet or onto the carpet where we slept. My slogan now became *Yêu không đam mê thì đừng yêu; uống mà không say thì đừng uống*. As love without passion is not love, so drinking alcohol without getting drunk or passing out is not good drinking.

I had the feeling I was heading for destruction, but while I recognized the danger, I was powerless against my trauma, sadness and sense of vulnerability about the future. I was trying to escape reality.

In our parties there were always fights about little things, because alcohol makes people talkative and aggressive. When anyone became belligerent, our strategy was to give him more drink until he passed out. "Hey, let's drink and *then* talk! Only when you take one more full cup will we be able trust what you're talking about!" We constantly talked about the same things, like we were endlessly rewinding and replaying the same scene in an old video and commenting on it. No one was able to listen and nothing was resolved.

We weren't getting anywhere besides making ourselves sick. More alcohol and more talk often gave me terrible headaches. There were times I hugged the toilet bowl more than anything else. Sometimes we didn't even know where the toilet was and just vomited and wallowed in it. What a waste of money and lives.

Loneliness, isolation and depression began to sink in. Not one of us realized that we were all traumatized by the past, and no one knew the way to get free. We were sinking in the quicksand, slowly killing ourselves in denial.

I began to look for a way out. I had to get out totally and make new friends with people I could trust and rely on. I could not remain with a group of people who only knew about work, drink, vomit and swearing. In the back of my mind I still knew that God had not rescued me from the Khmer Rouge prison for this senseless debauchery.

But my life was like a small boat on the great ocean, lost

without a compass or even a paddle. I was adrift and did not know what to do to rebuild my self-confidence. I feared being hit by the tidal wave of reality. I dreamed of living a normal life, of moving forward, but forward to what goal? Forward to what purpose? Under the hardship of prison and torture my purpose was to survive; in the refugee camp it was to study and work to gain a chance to resettle in a third country. In both places the crying from within was suppressed. Only now, when loneliness and lovesickness had triggered the troubled past, had it risen up to swamp me.

I had been physically and mentally fit, and it was this that enabled me to survive under the toughest conditions. But in this affluent society, that fitness didn't seem to have any worth. In Phanat Nikhom, I had sincerely promised myself that when I came to Australia, I would rebuild my life in appreciation for the opportunity this new country was giving me. But it is always easier to make a promise to oneself than to carry it out. My emotions were like small stones in the desert being buried again by the sands of trouble. I felt an utter failure, and I began to wonder whether I was normal enough to have a family. I had no solid foundation on which to build my life, so all my attempts were futile. I had the will to survive the toughest conditions, but not the will, or the means, to live a brand new life.

I often laughed and asked myself in a pessimistic tone, "Is there any meaning in living? Is there any worth in life without alcohol?" It was a cry of a broken spirit.

It all came to a head on the first anniversary of my arrival in Australia. We threw a party to celebrate. That night I drank excessively and slept in a pool of my own vomit. The next morning when I woke I had a severe headache. My hair was stuck together with dried vomit and the smell was horrible. As I went to the bathroom to clean up, I felt deeply ashamed of my foolishness. I saw the others had the same problem, and the thought brought me to my senses. The Khmer Rouge chained me to a big tree and I wallowed in mud to survive, but here there was no tree, no chain. Yet I was in a virtual prison, wallowing in stupidity. I was determined to get out.

I was convinced I needed special guidance so that I could find the courage and strength to make a good choice and be single-minded about it. But where could I find it? Alcohol, work, my old lifestyle and my unresolved problems had taken me away from God. The community of faith was still there, available to welcome me despite everything. Many Sundays I went to the church service half drunk. I didn't know how bad I smelt. Yet when I realized I was on the road to destruction, I earnestly looked up to God and prayed, again with the desperation I had in the Cambodian jungle.

"Lord, please show me the way out this sea of turbulence! Please give me the courage to change and bail me out of this cycle of pain and gradual death!"

Throughout this time Lyn had faithfully maintained our friendship. She frequently came to visit me and my friends. Sometimes I even told her, "I wish you were a boy so you could drink with us and sleep here. Then I could talk to you more. But you're a girl so you can't." She smiled but said nothing. I did not understand that such a comment would probably hurt any girl deeply.

Because I still considered Lan my girlfriend during my early days in Australia, I didn't want to get close to any other woman. I didn't want to be a traitor to my own heart or cheat on someone I loved. Her absence made me even more careful with the opposite sex. I would not violate Lan's trust. The traditional Confucian moral code, passed on to me by my father, dictated that boys and girls could not be close in simple friendship. I didn't want to get any closer to Lyn because I feared the relationship might go too far or send her the wrong message. That was the reason why I wished she was a boy who could party with us. I also wanted a sensible person to talk to, someone with a clearer mind than my friends and me. I was desperately looking for a way out.

Lyn must have had good eyes because she saw clearly that we were a bunch of young men running away from life through alcohol. She didn't mind sitting in on our parties sometimes, but she never touched any of the exotic food or alcohol. If someone offered it to her, she greeted the invitation with a broad smile and a firm, "No thanks." Even in my drinking madness, this increased my admiration for her, but I never confessed this to her. No one ever dared to abuse her or say anything bad about her because all my friends knew she was special to me.

"She has something that we totally lack, some inner strength," I told the boys. It was humiliating for us tough guys—especially me, the hardest drinking guy at all the parties—to admit that a skinny young woman had more strength than we did, but it was true. She had the courage to come, sit with us and befriend us, yet not let us influence her by our way of living.

"Do you *like* drinking?" she would often ask me. With others I might attempt to cover up, but somehow with Lyn, out of my respect for her as a friend, I could not. Over many months I had found her to be someone who could be trusted.

"No! I truly don't like drinking!" I would confess abruptly without looking at her. "But drinking gives me some release to ease my pain!"

"What pain?" she would ask naively, her sweet tone pleading for an answer.

Often I gave a smile of denial and counseled myself, "If you ever share the pain, she won't handle it." The betrayal, the nightmares, the torture, the trauma, the heartbreak of losing Lan—all this I felt I was supposed to endure silently. "The pain will go with me to the grave," I often told myself.

I also feared that if I shared with her about my past, especially Lan's rejection, I would not be emotionally strong enough and would cry in front of her. For years I had painted myself as a tough soldier, so to break down in tears before a girl would be the end of the world. I could not accept it.

But Lyn persevered. The words I probably heard most often from her lips were, "You need God, and you need a new life in Christ. He can heal you!" At first it was like water off a duck's back. I knew deep down that I needed a new life, but how do you start? That was the question I hadn't answered, and that was why I was in such a mess. I couldn't tell her this because 'soldiers are tough'. This was one of the most delusional aspects of my pride, and it was the very thing that was killing me, as it kills many pretentious men.

One thing her repeated statement achieved, however, was to

remind me about God and His church. I had accepted the Lord Jesus a few months earlier in a superficial way, but I had not developed a solid relationship with Him. I read the Bible now and then, but words alone kill; it is the Spirit who gives life. I still, foolishly, could not accept the miracles of the Gospels, thinking they were mere propaganda. "We live in a scientific age, not a superstitious one," I reasoned. The materialism of Marxist-Leninist theory was still a stumbling block to me.

There were parts of the Bible I still enjoyed reading, though, especially the books of Proverbs and Ecclesiastes. Through them God continued to touch me. Gradually the Word began to come alive to me. Proverbs, which I had read before, now gave me something new to grasp onto in this crisis. Among other things I read:

Who has woe? Who has sorrow?
  Who has strife? Who has complaints?
  Who has needless bruises? Who has bloodshot eyes?
Those who linger over wine,
  who go to sample bowls of mixed wine.
Do not gaze at wine when it is red,
  when it sparkles in the cup,
  when it goes down smoothly!
In the end it bites like a snake
  and poisons like a viper.
Your eyes will see strange sights,
  and your mind will imagine confusing things.
You will be like one sleeping on the high seas,
  lying on top of the rigging.
"They hit me," you will say, "but I'm not hurt!
  They beat me, but I don't feel it!
When will I wake up
  so I can find another drink?" (Proverbs 23:29–35)

How accurately did these words described my way of life in those days. I had read them before yet without any sense of conviction. Now I was convinced that I needed to be seriously committed to life—and to Christ—again.

The desire to change, as well as seeing that there was something genuine in the people of faith, urged me to step out and try a new thing. I needed to mean business with this Lord whom I once had professed to embrace. I needed to let His Spirit consolidate my faith in Him and be single-minded about Him, rather than half-hearted and dismissive of Him and His work as simply an 'intelligent faith'.

One Friday evening Lyn said gently to me, "This coming Sunday, the pastor from my New Zealand church will be visiting. Can you come to the service earlier than usual?"

"Yes, I will come early," I promised without hesitation.

Because of this commitment, for the first time ever I refused to drink with the boys the following night. "I want to go to church clean tomorrow," I told them.

"What! Did you say you want to be clean for church tomorrow?" They all burst into laughter. They knew someone who drank like me couldn't just stop overnight.

"Yeah!" one yelled. "You'll go to church tomorrow and be changed into a saint!"

Someone walked to the fridge, took out a bottle of milk, poured it into a large cup and handed it to me. With a smirk on his face he said sarcastically, "Mate! Real men drink beer; babies drink milk!"

Normally an insult like that would have started an argument, but that night I thought, "I'd better give in to him. A fight won't change the situation." I was truly offended by him, but I fought to keep my promise and hold to my desire to change. I mustered my self-control. "I've been in this house with them, drinking together, for months," I told myself. "We all like to have fun, and of course they need something to laugh at. Tonight is the night they can make fun of me."

That evening I went to sleep earlier than normal. I had decided that if I had any hint of an opportunity to change my way of living, I would single-mindedly embrace it. No longer was I driven by the need to prove myself to others; I didn't care what the boys thought of me. They had no power over me. I needed to begin a new life.

I have never regretted the decision I made that night. It was during that Sunday morning service that the prophetic word which began this book came directly to me through the New Zealand pastor, Peter Morrow. The Lord hit me right on the spot and nailed me. I was absolutely stunned. How on earth could this total stranger know about my past? It was unbelievable, but the unbelievable was confronting me forcefully.

With my sleeping habits, everyone knew that before the service was half over I was usually off in dreamland, no matter how good or lively the preaching was. But that Sunday morning I didn't have a chance to sleep. The prophetic word captured me and held me on a knife's edge. The secrets of my past were being named openly by someone who couldn't possibly have known them: "mouth gasping for air . . . nightmares . . . betrayal . . . " My time in the army, my horrific experiences of torture, the lying to survive, the desire to run away from reality—I had told no one of these things. In our drinking parties, others talked, but I just drank until I passed out. I was sure all my dark secrets would die with me.

Yet all of this hidden past was unveiled that morning. And that scared me.

My first reaction to the prophetic word that day was very negative. I immediately walked into the garden at the back of the house, feeling more comfortable with the vegetables than the people inside. But my reaction proved that God had shot his arrow into the right target. Deep down I knew the truth, that God had revealed His knowledge of me through His servant. I was totally convicted.

But if an unbeliever or someone who does not understand comes in while everybody is prophesying, he will be convinced by all that he is a sinner and will be judged by all, and the secrets of his heart will be laid bare. So he will fall down and worship God, exclaiming, "God is really among you!" (1 Corinthians 14:24–25)

Because of the accuracy of the prophetic word, I later accused Lyn of telling Peter Morrow about me. But the reality was I had never shared these details of my life with her (and she was not the type of person to gossip anyway). The conviction of this word of prophecy was a strong stimulant to my drowsy heart, and I repented genuinely from all the problems in my life. From that platform of repentance, I also sincerely gave the Lord God room to change my life.

God's work is solid, and he often confirms what he is doing. A few weeks after this meeting, another visiting pastor delivered almost the same message about my secret past and my future. I knew then I could not run from God. The warning was severe: if I continued along the path I had been following, I would get into even more serious trouble.

Anyone who says they don't have fear is either lying or out of touch with personal sensibility. I knew fear—the fear of imprisonment and torture, the fear of revisiting my miserable life in the refugee camp with its malaria, alcohol and betrayal. I never wanted to go back to such scenes again.

But God was with me. He had saved me. I had seen His light in the dream as a child. I had heard His voice through the urging within my spirit. I had felt His conviction in His Word, and it was like water when I was lost in the jungle. Now God had spoken again to revive my dying soul here in Australia.

Chapter twenty-one

THE JOY OF KNOWING HIM

Truly I say to you, You will be weeping and sorrowing, but the world will be glad: you will be sad, but your sorrow will be turned into joy. (John 16:20 BBE)

The Lord's aim is to give us His joy, yet to get this joy in my life I have found there have never been any short cuts. It is not merely about intellectually understanding the Bible. It is about being saturated with His Spirit, and then He brings the inner joy. When I accepted Christ as my personal Savior, I gave Him a signal that there was room in my heart for Him to dwell. He came in and opened my heart and mind. Moreover, I could understand Him and receive His peace.

It took me quite a long time to grasp the crux of the joy of the Lord in my life. Perhaps I was a slow learner, or perhaps it was the hardening of my heart from life's experiences. Only the Lord knew when the perfect time was for me to understand Him. It was a slow process, yet the effect was long lasting, and I preferred it that way.

After becoming a believer, I intended to live a pure life. However, the more I tried in my own strength, the less successful I was. While attempting to live a holy life I was satisfied on the outside, but inwardly it was still war and strife. To please the Lord and to live the way of my Savior, I had to allow the Spirit of God to help clean me up from the inside.

How foolish I was in thinking I could live to His standard through my own strength! I may have had a strong will to live in the jungle and in imprisonment, but I could not follow the Lord's way of holiness through sheer determination. What a wretch I was, for I had no idea about the grace of God. I had no idea about the work of the Holy Spirit. I didn't understand the simplicity of "walking with Him" (Galatians 5:16, 22). I wanted to work for Him, but my Lord desired me to work *alongside* Him. I wanted to be His slave and prisoner, but He said, "I have called you friend" (John 15:15). Those discoveries were truly the most effective moments in my spiritual and emotional walk.

"We're going to have a baptism class," our pastor, David Boyd, said at a BBQ one Sunday after the service. "How many of you want to take it and be baptized this time?"

There were four newly born-again Christians in the small church, including me. An ex-Catholic Filipino girl and two Vietnamese, one from a strong Buddhist background, raised their hands, but as usual I was as stubborn as a mule and said nothing. Three months or so had passed since the day God touched my life through Peter Morrow, but I still felt shy about my conversion.

The three others turned around and looked at me. "What about you, Uong? Are you also going to attend the class and get baptized with us?" I couldn't resist the smiling invitation of those friendly people.

As the pastor of the church, David conducted the Bible studies prior to the baptism. "You have to understand what the Bible teaches about water baptism, and you must know what you're doing." Other older Christians in the leadership team underlined this. David showed us many Bible verses and enthusiastically explained what they meant. We memorized some verses, especially from Romans 6.

Did I understand it all? Not really! I may have learnt all the verses by heart, but as for grasping their importance I was still miles off. Because I had agreed to do it, however, I followed through in good faith. All I wanted to do was to please my Savior, even if I didn't fully understand the spiritual significance of it all.

It proved to be a well-timed decision. Every step I took towards God, He strode five or more towards me with gladness in His heart.

On the Saturday afternoon of the baptism, we had to use another church's facility because our church didn't have a baptismal pool. I was to be baptized last, so I'd prepared my personal testimony well. There were a lot of worship songs, a few of which will stay with me for the rest of my life. As I was being totally submerged in the cold water, my whole body began to shake. I didn't know if it was the winter coldness or the presence of God that made me tremble that way. But as my Christian brothers and sisters witnessed the transforming miracle of God, they all began to sing:

I'm a new creation, I'm brand new man,
All things have passed away, I've been born again,
More than a conqueror, that's who I am.
I'm a new creation; I'm a brand new man.

As that song drew to a close someone began to read loudly the beautiful verses from Romans 6:

Since we have died to sin, how can we continue to live in it? Or have you forgotten that when we became Christians and were baptized to become one with Christ Jesus, we died with him? For we died and were buried with Christ by baptism. And just as Christ was raised from the dead by the glorious power of the Father, now we also may live new lives.

Since we have been united with him in his death, we will also be raised as he was. Our old sinful selves were crucified with Christ so that sin might lose its power in our lives. We are no longer slaves to sin. For when we died with Christ we were set free from the power of sin. And since we died with Christ, we know we will also share his new life. We are sure of this because Christ rose from the dead, and he will never die again. Death no longer has any power over him. He died once to defeat sin, and now he lives for the glory of God. So you should consider yourselves dead to sin and able to live for the glory of God through Christ Jesus. (Romans 6:2–11 NLT)

It was like the Lord wanted to show me what was happening spiritually to me at that moment. Someone else prophesied, "From here you will go on experiencing a brand new life," then immediately another scripture was given:

Therefore, if anyone is in Christ, he is a new creation; the old has gone, the new has come! (2 Corinthians 5:17)

Yes, a brand new life was what I truly expected from God. I had learnt these verses prior to the baptism, but hearing them that day impacted me greatly. Suddenly I felt the warmth of tears slowly flowing from my dry eyes. Tears that I had lost for so many years had now come back in baptism. The Lord had restored them. I suddenly felt the love of God, specific, clear, and inarguable. I wasn't the type of person who allowed emotions to rule my life, but the conviction of His presence was so strong that day I could not withstand it.

At that point, I also realized I was among genuine believers of God. I had never felt this way before. I had not felt such genuine love and affection since I'd left my home in Vietnam. The Lord's presence and the love of His people touched me to the core.

As I was standing in the water—standing in God's presence— one of the young men began singing another faith song:

It's no longer I that liveth, but Christ that liveth in me,
It's no longer I that liveth, but Christ that liveth in me.
He lives, He lives—Jesus is alive in me!
It's no longer I that liveth, but Christ that liveth in me.

People joined in and repeated those words from Galatians 2:20 several times. More tears flowed. I couldn't control them.

I deeply appreciated those worship songs. They were more than mere words; they were scriptures recited to my heart and mind. The sound of them was so sweet. According to the Scriptures, I thought, it is not I who lives but Christ who lives in me, and he will change my life for good, forever. Those songs were more beautiful than the lullabies a mother in Vietnam sings to her infant, although that baby will remember them all his life. Those songs of Scripture, bright and meaningful, struck a deep nerve. They became a strong and solid foundation for my earliest transformation into a Christian life. They taught me that I could only live a new life in Christ as I trusted in Him.

I recognized it was a burial service for me in that cold pool. Now, after many years, I understand that if I desire a brand new life, I must go through a true burial. The old life in me must die as I allow the new, indestructible seed of the Gospel of God to germinate. Then the brand new life has room to grow and mature.

After that day, the joy kept flowing in my heart. Before turning to Christ I stored up hatred and pain, but during the baptism I experienced something beyond human touch. It was the Lord performing surgery on my innermost being, yet without the pain I had endured years before when my uncle operated on me to remove shrapnel from the explosion that killed my friend Tai. The manifestation of Christ's life in me was so tangible that I now knew without a doubt where my life was heading—towards Him.

I thought back over the emptiness that had haunted me for so long. I had never known what I was longing for. I didn't realize that these feelings were intended to prompt me to search for something more meaningful. I *had* searched, but in all the wrong places. But now through Christ I could call God 'Father'. The emptiness, the isolation, the disconnectedness came from a lack of relationship with the Creator God.

How easy it is to acknowledge God yet still not see Him at work to bring about the joy of life! I had learnt the hard lesson of repentance and admitted my pride, my 'can do' attitude and my refusal to be vulnerable before Him. He helped rid me of my thick layer of self-protection. The more completely my sin was exposed, the more thoroughly the Holy Spirit could deal with it. When all my efforts to put up barriers against life and God were unmasked and unpacked, at last I came closer to Him.

The Sunday service on the day after my water baptism was so touching and the worship so alive. We sang:
The steadfast love of the Lord never ceases,
His mercies never come to an end,
They are new every morning, new every morning,
Great is Thy faithfulness, O Lord,
Great is Thy faithfulness.
Another song followed:
Put on the garment of praise for the spirit of heaviness . . .
The whole church danced with all their might. The wooden floors in the house shook. I sat in the back seat feeling embarrassed for these people, but as they sang and danced, enjoying God's presence, I opened my eyes and looked up. Everyone was reveling in God, and I began to feel a bit envious.

Why shouldn't I have what they have? I thought. As I looked closely at myself, it came as a surprise: *I* was the boring person, not them. *I* was the dead fish. *I* was the one with the problems, not them. I shouldn't criticize them for enjoying the presence of God. Why didn't I join in and enjoy God as well?

Previously, when everyone was worshiping God in church, I had not wholeheartedly participated. "It isn't my style," was my line of defense. But now I felt a new urge from within. I started to see worship through different eyes. I used to think the singing wasn't that great, but now a desire to worship God as the others did was born.

"I won't be critical anymore," I promised myself that day. "I will come to church and worship God and be excited with Him just as these Christians are." As I kept the promise, the Lord seemed to have more room to move in my life to usher in transformation. This I later understood to be the principle of being proactive with God so I could receive more blessings and grow more mature. Eventually I learnt that the desire to worship is the most wonderful part of God taking the initiative in my heart:

Delight yourself in the LORD and he will give you the desires of your heart. (Psalm 37:4)

The sermon that first Sunday after my baptism was also wonderful. I found I could understand more of the preaching. It was probably the first time I had ever sat through the whole sermon without sleeping! I still remember the text: Luke 17:11–19, the story of the ten lepers who were healed by Jesus. All of them were healed as they obeyed the Lord and walked off to find the priest. Yet only one, a foreigner, came back to worship Christ that day.

The story touched me deeply. "Will I be like those nine healed lepers, ungrateful for what Christ has done?" I asked myself. "Will I be so focused on my own life, that I forget to bring praise and thanks to the Lord my God? Or will I be like that foreigner— healed and walking away, like the rest of them, but then turning back to praise and worship Jesus the healer?"

I said a quiet prayer that day: "Lord, give me strength and always remind me to thank you, to give you praise, and to worship you."

The church service finished with a well-known song:

Something beautiful, something good
All my confusion He understood
All I had to offer Him was brokenness and strife
But He made something beautiful of my life

I felt immensely moved by these lyrics. I could identify with the composer. I had nothing to offer God besides my wounds, my bruises, my brokenness, my hatred and the trauma of war and imprisonment. However, God, with His master touch, restored me, fulfilled His promise and poured into my heart His joy. He made me a brand-new creation in His eyes. If I was born empty and had travelled through life with bruises, the Lord my God had guided my every step until He could fill me.

My tears again ran freely that morning.

Chapter twenty-two

JOY AND FORGIVENESS

My growing experience of worship opened up a whole new world to me. When I sang and worshipped God, I felt joy, and this joy of the Lord drew me further on to walk with Him. It was like the beautiful dream of light I had when I was ten, but it could never be taken away from me. In Christ I could be fulfilled—and more than that, I could come into God's presence. In worshiping Him truly, from the depths of my heart, I allowed the Spirit of God to enter, and, with Christ's blood and Word, to wash away my past.

I felt a sense of joy in the eternal. Everything God is and does is marked by joy, and that joy is pure because He is pure. In turn His joy creates in *us* a desire to be pure. In a nutshell, life is about joy. But somehow the enemies of God and the blindness of mankind have combined to prevent us from having the best. Jesus Christ became a Message and has touched billions of people throughout the ages so that His joy could become theirs, by grace. And now I was among them.

The Spirit of God illuminated the work of the Savior in me and brought me to understand the kernel of the Message and see the value of my life in His life and work. I began to understand the term 'in Christ'. I am now grafted into Him, like a body part that a surgeon transplants into somebody in need. The part grafted in now lives by blood from the recipient's heart. God's heart-blood is forgiveness. With my life now grafted into Christ's, I needed the same compassion and forgiving spirit as He has. This knowledge is my joy, a kind that human language is inadequate to describe. The early apostles called it 'inexpressible joy' (1 Peter 1:8).

As I kept reading through the book of Acts, I found that the early church not only preached about Christ and His resurrection but also said much about joy in the Holy Spirit. The Spirit enabled them to experience joy even in the midst of severe persecution. Even when some were killed, that suffering could not quench their feelings. I often wonder what it took for Paul, Peter and the other apostles, who professed that they forsook everything for Him, to know Christ. To understand the heart, the whole counsel, of God in the person of Jesus Christ was their ultimate joy.

Many times in my life I had been set free, and each time I'd had some joy. When I knew I was free from the death camp of the Khmer Rouge, it was exhilarating. When I was delivered from the Thai military prison, it was wonderful. When I was accepted by the Australian delegation to come to Australia, it was a time of celebration. But none of these experiences can compare with what I have in Christ. Jesus promised His joy was something that no one could take away from those who believed in Him (John 16:22).

The joy that the world offered me had its effect, but it was short-lived. I ended up in depression, despair and drunkenness. The joy I have in the Lord God has a lasting effect. I have seen my life transformed, and there is no way I could have done it apart from God. Christ, His Word and the presence of His Spirit generated in me a deep sense of happiness.

As I became more established in that exuberant young church through solid biblical teaching and genuine fellowship, I gained more trust in God and His people. My confidence again flourished. I began to grasp the centrality of the church's activities: to worship God and to carry out His love and work in the world. Gradually, I also understood that God's perfect gift is "pure joy" even in trials (James 1:2). God had allowed all the trials I had experienced, and now He was waiting for me to make a choice and move towards forgiveness and joy. He wanted to see whether I was truly in Christ with joy or had merely adopted religion to cover up my bitterness. In Christ's name, I began to let the old wounds go. I could never allow them to pull me down so that I could not function as a healthy member in His body.

The first of the victories of Christ in me was that I could forgive my enemies, my betrayer and my torturers. It took quite a while before I understood the principle of forgiveness and its benefit for my relationship with God, my wholeness and my ability to function in the church and society around me. In the end it was God's victory alone. The Spirit of Christ enlivened His good gift in me. I knew He forgave my nasty youth; He canceled all my offences against Him so that I in turn could forgive all those who had offended against or intentionally set out to destroy me. It is easy for us to parrot the Christian creed and say, "I believe in the forgiveness of sins," but in my case my belief became reality.

To forgive my betrayer and torturers was never an easy task, but God gave me the joy so I had His strength to carry out this work.

First I learnt how to show forgiveness to Dung Map, my betrayer, for pointing a gun full of bullets at me and ordering me to retrieve a radio during the ambush. My prayer in those days was: "Lord, please increase my faith and strength so that I can forgive Dung." It was not about simply quoting the Bible but actually standing on the promise the Lord gave to Paul: "My grace is sufficient for you" (2 Corinthians 12:9). His grace, which produced the joy I experienced after my baptism, allowed me to say to God, "Yes, I can do it. I can forgive Dung. In Christ's name, I refuse to hate him."

During the times of interrogation and severe torture by the Khmer Rouge, every time I woke up after passing out, my heart was filled with anger and hatred towards Dung. And not just him but his entire family. The rage and loathing were indescribable. My feelings towards the Khmer Rouge had the sense of, "If I get out of here I will come back and level you all," yet this could not compare with my bitterness towards Dung. Had the Khmer Rouge understood the state of my mind in those days, instead of torturing me they could have treated my wounds, fed me well, equipped me with a weapon and sent me home. I would have killed Dung and all his family to satisfy the hatred that boiled within.

Prior to my conversion, and especially prior to my baptism, I had tried to bury the issue of Dung and the resentment he caused. But I dealt with it in my own way, sweeping it under the carpet, pretending it wasn't there. I felt that 'time would heal' but it didn't. Often I had emotional outbursts with no idea where they came from or why they were happening. Out of the blue I would feel a sudden rage; or, if somebody said or did something that might cause me resentment, emotions would rise with the full force of anger.

I discovered that to forgive someone like Dung is another form of suffering and agony, because every time I thought about him there was this turmoil within and I had shortened breath. But as I confessed to the Lord that He was my God, I began to rely on Him to deal with the issue. Every morning after I got up, I looked into the mirror and professed, "In Christ Jesus I forgive Dung Map. God, please give me the strength to carry out this life of forgiveness. I want to forgive like you have forgiven all people, even your enemies who crucified you on the cross." Over time I felt less intense when I thought about Dung. It was a real joy to experience this victory in the name of Jesus.

Next I had to learn to forgive the Khmer Rouge. Towards Boong Chian, Oum Uot, and the others who had tortured and tried to kill me, I felt hatred. But my most searing feelings were directed towards Dhara, the young boy who made my life hell. He was the person I found hardest to forgive and forget. I had to pray to the Lord to increase my faith and strengthen my inner man before I was able to forgive these men. The vivid memories of their murderous acts were often the cause of nightmares and disturbances to my sleep. I thought about them often, and every time my body broke into a cold sweat and I felt the chills.

Indeed, I sweated and shook a lot as I wrestled with forgiving these enemies. As I came to know more about being created in God's image, I realized that the Lord demanded I should be master over many things (Genesis 1:26), including the bitterness within. To follow Him meant to imitate Him and be gracious to my foes in order to reflect Him in my life. I further discovered there was a link between forgiveness and answered prayer. Christ's words struck me to the core:

I tell you the truth, if anyone says to this mountain, "Go, throw yourself into the sea," and does not doubt in his heart but believes that what he says will happen, it will be done for him. Therefore I tell you, whatever you ask for in prayer, believe that you have received it, and it will be yours. And when you stand praying, if you hold anything against anyone, forgive him, so that your Father in heaven may forgive you your sins. (Mark 11:23–25)

God's principle hit me clearly: if I didn't forgive my enemies, my prayers would find no answer. I wanted my prayers to be heard, so I concluded that the boiling from within must not be a mountain that barricaded me from having my Father answer me.

At one point I thought forgiving these people was impossible, but the Lord prompted my memory so that each time unforgiveness rose, I was reminded of what I had done to people in my village and how I had hurt many of them, especially the Communist Party member and his family. I was also reminded of the two Bibles I had ripped apart in the refugee camp. God forgave me all and gave me His joy; at the same time He empowered me to do the impossible thing and forgive the unforgivable. It was the ultimate joy when I discovered that with Christ and His forgiving Spirit I could do it.

God does have a sense of humor. He even tested whether I had truly forgiven. Towards the end of 1991, the door suddenly opened for my friend Lyn and me to be involved in prison ministry. To my amazement, the first person God allowed us to reach out to was a Cambodian gangster. He became a believer in Christ after a few visits, and how the Lord increased my joy! I then knew I was truly free from bitterness and hatred.

After forgiveness, the second important discovery of my joy was being freed from past knowledge. Over many years, Vietnamese culture had blended three major Eastern religions—Buddhism, Confucianism and Taoism—into its national psyche, as well as ancestral worship. In modern times, Marxist-Leninism and nationalism were also included. This created a cultic experience for many. To be free from this, to unlearn what I had learnt in the past, I needed the power of God.

Previously I had no problem with reading the entire Bible,

especially Ecclesiastes, Proverbs, and Psalms, but I had intentionally avoided and rejected the miracles recorded in the New Testament. I believed they were fabrications, like traditional legends; I thought I could simply enjoy the Bible's moral teaching. It was David Boyd, a student of science as well as a pastor, who challenged my thinking about this. We set out a time to systematically study the Scriptures together, challenging each other's thoughts. He earned my respect and I allowed him to influence me greatly.

The first two years of my Christian life were critical. Many times David and I talked openly about all aspects of life and belief. I came to realize my presumptions and prejudices were wrong. New thoughts poured through my mind. Why were so many of the greatest thinkers of the world from the Western part of the globe? Sir Isaac Newton, my hero, and a host of other Christian thinkers, along with great writers such as Pushkin and Leo Tolstoy, were not naive. The fathers of modern thinking such as Darwin and Marx, even though fallen from grace, once studied at Christian schools and no doubt were influenced by them.

I loved education, but at the same time I had been a victim of it under the Communist utopia. David was very supportive as I fought to counter my early indoctrination. "Read the Gospels, young man," he said. "Read the Gospels, pray about the passage, and don't rely on your own understanding."

I began to read the Bible, not as a book of literature anymore, but as a manual for knowing God and living practically. I found new joy in reading about the ministry of Jesus Christ. The Lord God chipped away, day by day, and allowed me to look into His glory and understand life in Him rather than life in science. I still loved reading science books, but only to update myself about recent discoveries. I began to understand the miracles from the Gospel's angle and appreciate them.

Then one day it occurred to me: "If miracles don't happen, then how did I find water in the dry jungle of Cambodia when I was wounded, dehydrated and almost dead?" I could not answer that. "Why did the pool of water contain only six or seven liters? If it had been more, I might have stayed there, exhausted, and died beside the pool." I could not answer that either. Above all I asked myself, "How did I survive the Khmer Rouge and all that torture? How did I survive the malaria that attacked me again and again?" I felt sure it wasn't just luck. Only the Lord God and His miracles had sustained my life. I realized that miracles happen, but I had been blinded by the presumptions of a quasi-scientific view of the world and had allowed this to squeeze the Lord God out of my life.

I was healed from many things, but the most wonderful healing was from my cultic presumption that science is all we have. By overcoming this prejudice, I embraced the Gospel more deeply as the message of God for my life.

Another undeniable joy was that I was now free from the desire to run away from life. Prior to my water baptism and encounter with the Holy Spirit, I had wanted to drown my life with alcohol, but the next morning I'd get up with headaches and wish I could live somewhere far away from society. This desire to run was rooted in the fear of being betrayed and hurt again. Moreover, it is part of the Vietnamese national psyche that when things get tough we prefer to live as an *ẩn dật* (recluse). I had that feeling.

Sometimes I probed Lyn: "I want to live on the moon or in the desert, in some quiet place that has no contact with other human beings. Will you come with me?" Thankfully she stood her ground and wouldn't compromise. She knew what she was called to. "God is calling me to be the light of the world, not to run away," she said. "You can have true peace right here and live and challenge the world."

I admired her for that courage and wished I had the same inner peace. And my desire came true as the Lord gave me the joy to live, the joy of knowing that He is here and still leads His people in whatever circumstances they go through.

Knowing the Creator, the mastermind behind all things, and seeing Him as a personal friend is truly an awesome reality. Through Jesus I can access God at any time without hindrance. This was mind-boggling to me at first, but now I embrace it. Through His Spirit I can feel Him, sense His presence and know He is in control. That is the real joy of my life. Tears still come every time I share this knowledge because He allows me to walk beside Him and work with Him. Who wouldn't have this joy when they see this reality?

As a soldier lost in the jungle, my desire was to return to base, rejoin the army fold, confess my failure and bear any consequences. The Lord had more in mind than that. He brought me back to the real fold by giving me a relationship between a Father and a son. Also he gave me the joy of being in His presence, with many other believers in the world.

Am I a dreamer? Absolutely not. I am planted in a solid reality, and this helped usher in the transformation of my life.

Chapter twenty-three

TRANSFORMATION

Neither circumcision nor uncircumcision means anything; what
counts is a new creation. (Galatians 6:15)

I had a desire to be more than just a believer who went to church
on Sunday mornings and warmed a seat. The Lord did not want
me to be just a religious person. He wanted me to be transformed
in Him through the work of the Holy Spirit.

As a young Christian I had no idea who the Holy Spirit was.
I only paid lip service to him when thinking about the Godhead.
Lack of knowledge made me live a fickle life. The first year of my
Christian walk was full of ups and downs, and many times I tried
to quit the church altogether. I had made a commitment to the Lord
to be in the church services, but commitment without love, and
being in church without a passion for Christ, made my connection
with Him very shallow.

In the services and Bible studies, David and the other leaders
mentioned quite a lot about the Holy Spirit and His work in
revealing Jesus to us. "Who is this person anyway?" I asked myself.
"And why do the people in church weirdly 'speak in tongues'?" It
was a totally strange sound to me and a bit of an annoyance when
we entered the worship time. Once again, however, the problem
wasn't them; it was me because I had no idea of the Holy Spirit
and His gifts.

In the summer of 1991 the church held a retreat in the Blue
Mountains, and there I gave in to the power of the Holy Spirit.

Like the wind that gently blows, the Spirit of God met me and empowered me in His own way (John 3:8). The most important thing was that He gained a free hand to revive a dead person. The torture of the Khmer Rouge and Thai military intelligence could not crack my shield of logical thinking, but the Lord God was more than able to by injecting His Spirit into my soul.

The impact was immediate. I went home from the retreat and my Bible reading increased dramatically. It seemed as if the Word held a different dimension for me. The Bible became more like solid food and brought more clarity to my thinking than ever before.

Lyn saw I was a man who enjoyed reading so she bought me books. It reminded me a lot of Vien, my third sister, who realized I was having trouble in my early teens and brought home numerous books for me to read. Reading the Bible and other Christian literature helped deepen my conviction of God's work.

I treasured certain verses highly, among them Psalm 32:1–2:

Happy is he who has forgiveness for his wrongdoing, and whose sin is covered. Happy is the man in whom the Lord sees no evil, and in whose spirit there is no deceit. (BBE)

I now understood what it was to have my sin covered, to be cleansed by the washing of Jesus' blood. The change came by God's power alone, and that made me happy because I was powerless to put my life together, let alone carry out the task of cleansing my soul.

One Sunday over lunch, David began to ask me more specific questions. "Uong, can you tell me about your life?"

Immediately my long-standing defensive mechanism kicked in. *Oh no! He's touching the sacred cow! Nobody has any right to know about my past. Nobody is going to know about the betrayal of my friend and leader. No one is going to know the army communication codes. The lies I told the Khmer Rouge and Thai military intelligence to survive will die with me.*

David had asked his question innocently, but I told him exactly what I had told the Khmer Rouge, the Thais and the rest of the world before.

This time, however, it was different. For weeks after I gave

David the details of my fake identity, I felt terribly convicted. My lies had given me mastery over the Khmer Rouge and Thai military intelligence, and I was secretly very proud about it. But somehow it was not the same with this innocent man. Instead of feeling good about the lying and cheating, I felt totally ashamed. Here was a man who had no martial arts skills, no club, no chain, no torture techniques or intention to intimidate. All he wanted was to know about someone in his church so he could pray and take care of him more effectively. When he asked he had a genuine look, yet I had treated him the same way I treated my enemies.

The shame of this cowardice increased. "Why should I treat him that way?" I asked myself. "Do I have the courage and inner strength to tell the truth about my real self?" I knew I didn't. My lying was itself evidence that I had not embraced the inner strength and courage to confront my fears. Once again I was running away—from my real self.

The battle within kept raging. Even though this church was small, I had first come because it attracted me. At the time I had no idea whether it was the presence of God, or the friendliness and acceptance I felt there, or even the free lunch. But the people were genuine. I could see it in their eyes, and I knew I could trust them as I had found trust in my friend Lyn.

This line of thought troubled me even more. *They had the courage to accept me and allow me to become part of their community. How cowardly am I, intentionally lying to people who genuinely care, and even to a pastor? How could I do it?*

Trust is my fundamental nature, but war and betrayal had forced me to think I could never trust anybody again. In this case the people of the church had trusted me, but I hadn't trusted them. Without trust I could not be a healthy man. My conscience was touched by the Spirit of God, and the urge to come out into the light was strong.

For some time I considered an alternative idea: leaving the church. But I wasn't convinced. Yes, I could leave, but that would only be running away from reality again. When I was a failure in Year 6, I had tried to run away from it, but my father prevented me. He taught me a lesson about not running. I learnt more about not running in this painful way in my adult years. Now it was such an occasion again, but this time it was God who made me face myself.

How long will you keep running? my soul asked me, and I knew immediately that leaving was not the answer.

My thoughts kept accusing me. *If you keep lying, you won't have any chance to rebuild your life,* they told me during nights when I couldn't sleep. *If you keep on lying, when can you be real to yourself and to others? What about your future wife and family?* The idea of faking my identity with those close to me was hard to imagine. I couldn't be a fake with the ones I lived with for the rest of my life. *When will you trust again?* I knew without trust I would not have a happy life; the joy I had at present would only be a façade. *If you can't reveal your true identity, then you don't deserve the trust of the rest of the community.*

Worse still, the words of Jesus struck me between the eyes:

Woe to you, teachers of the law and Pharisees, you hypocrites! You give a tenth of your spices—mint, dill and cumin. But you have neglected the more important matters of the law—justice, mercy and faithfulness. You should have practiced the latter, without neglecting the former. You blind guides! You strain out a gnat but swallow a camel. (Matthew 23:23–24)

I was doing the outward religious things but neglecting more important matters. By cheating I was 'swallowing a camel'. I had pretended, and God didn't like it. I could not worship Him freely, could not identify with Christ freely, when my heart was held down by the darkness of cheating. As a result, my fellowship with the others in the church was blocked by a barrier and remained very shallow.

Verse after verse of the New Testament kept flowing through my mind. "Whoever follows me will never walk in darkness, but will have the light of life" (John 8:12). It was truly the kingdom of light invading the kingdom of darkness. I was the same as David when he cried out in the Psalms:

When I kept silent,
my bones wasted away
through my groaning all day long.

For day and night
  your hand was heavy upon me;
my strength was sapped
  as in the heat of summer.
Then I acknowledged my sin to you
  and did not cover up my iniquity.
I said, "I will confess
  my transgressions to the Lord"—
and you forgave
  the guilt of my sin. (Psalm 32:3–5)

No, I couldn't keep silent about my past anymore. Finally, after much fighting and consideration, to ease the conviction of the Holy Spirit's urging, I gave in. "Please, Lord," I prayed, "give me the courage to tell David, my close friend, about the whole of my life and the way I was. I want freedom from within so badly!" Faith needed action, and I concluded this would make me a mature person.

I rang David's home number to make an appointment. "Can I meet and have a serious talk with you sometime this week?"

As a pastor he treasured his people highly, so he agreed to meet in his home the next day. There I slowly revealed to him the truth: my fake identity, my wrong age, my fake birthplace and my involvement in a special military group.

David was stunned. He had not expected me to be so honest with him and willing to share the problems I had endured. But he appreciated my openness and the way I approached him with trust and honor.

"So you were a soldier in Cambodia and you were betrayed," he said. "You were also a prisoner of war in the Khmer Rouge! It must have been very tough for you. If it's okay, tell me more about your life . . ."

It was there in his house, for the first time, that I wholeheartedly shared my life and troubles with another person. I'm sure Lyn had already learnt some of it; my drinking buddies, who had been with me in Phanat Nikhom, knew about my imprisonment and sometimes blurted things out at our parties when she was there. But I had never shared with her what I shared with David that day.

Of course, I couldn't tell everything at once, for my story was a long one. But I shared the hardest things: the betrayal, the constant torture, the being buried alive and the many encounters with near death that the Lord allowed me to elude.

The importance of that day was that I dared to confront the powers of darkness and honestly expose my fake identity. I apologized to David for misleading him. To my amazement he did not judge or scold, but rather embraced me with understanding. The best thing was that after sharing my true identity and apologizing for 'swallowing a camel', I felt the burden was gone and replaced by an uplifted spirit.

God won a victory that day. He had urged me from within and enabled me to open myself up so that he could deepen the process of healing. The Spirit of God is in the business of restoring His people from the inside out. I found the courage and inner strength to confront my fears because I had freedom in Christ. That freedom gave me the strength to face the reality of life and not run away from it.

After I had shared with David, he insisted we have lunch together as normal. This allowed me to be at ease and assured me he accepted me even in my real identity. David and I remain friends to this day.

My experience of a convicted heart, along with the liberation of revealing myself to God and His people, was the real turning point in my spiritual walk. It was the platform for my total recovery from trauma. The Lord always wants to restore us, but we often limit Him by our failure to unpack our hearts. Of course we cannot unpack to everybody, but in God's congregation there are plenty of people we can trust and who are able to build us up to reflect Him who is in us.

Chapter twenty-four

THE JOY OF SERVING HIM

Better is one day in your courts than a thousand elsewhere; I would rather be a doorkeeper in the house of my God, than dwell in the tents of the wicked. (Psalms 84:10)

God had rescued me, and His intention was to bring about healing and restoration to my life. However, I wouldn't be healed totally, restored totally, or learn how to rely on Him totally unless I exercised the things He showed me in the Bible. Faith with action brings about the best in us as believers.

As a young man I enjoyed being active in whatever I did. Now, as a believer of Christ, my joy was to go about the Master's work. Knowing Him is serving Him. I had been a soldier, trained to be sent out and fight. God had now handpicked and trained me to fight other battles—not with flesh and blood but in the spiritual domain. As a soldier in the jungle I didn't have to have the presence of my commander to act. I was given a task to perform and only when the task was done was my assignment accomplished. In prison or under intense interrogation, even though I had left the armed forces years before, I still had the duty of protecting the information I had once been entrusted with. As a new convert, I switched my allegiance to God, and no doubt these principles from military service helped me in my spiritual journey.

Every time I engaged in a task, whether telling others about Jesus or just humbly serving them, I felt I was doing a good work that He had assigned to me. By acting out in faith I learnt a lot about the Lord, His provision, myself and my capacity in Him. I found plenty of joy in it.

The Bible showed me two things about this that I, as a former farmer, appreciated greatly. The first was that in Christ there is a time for everything—a time to rest and a time to take action (Ecclesiastes 3:1–12). The second was found in Deuteronomy 25:4: "Do not keep the ox from taking the grain when he is crushing it" (BBE). In the justice of God, even the animal that is working with man takes its share of the profit. I could never forget the animals working in the fields in Vietnam (mainly water buffalo). The farmers fed them while they were working by letting them help themselves while threshing the rice, beans or other farm produce. By the time the work was done, the animals were also filled with all the food they needed. Both man and animal rejoiced, for they had mutual benefit.

Salvation had been planted by God's Spirit, but the life of Christ in me needed room to grow. By being proactive with God and exercising His gifts, I became like an ox in His field. I found myself reveling in him, feeding on His love, enjoying both His rest and His work and being restored. I found answers to help others as well, for like the lady with the issue of blood (Luke 8:46–47), my Savior wanted me to be His witness. He comforted me so that I in turn could comfort others (2 Corinthians 1:4). God never wastes an opportunity.

Although I was still unwell with sporadic malaria attacks, and although I was still a young believer, the Lord said that I should move on in faith with Him and He would lead me to a more fulfilling and abundant life. If I held back and mollycoddled myself, I would not grow.

Whoever has a desire to keep his life, will have it taken from him; and whoever gives up his life because of me and the good news, will keep it. (Mark 8:35 BBE)

Our small Christian gathering kept growing in numbers, and the three-bedroom house where we met ran out of space. The leadership team saw the growth and decided to shift the church meeting to a nearby scout hall. On the Sunday afternoon two weeks before we were due to make the move, David said to me, "Hey, Uong! Can you come and give me a hand to mow the grass around the scout hall?"

I accepted without hesitation. The next Saturday morning I went over to his house early to start work.

The hall had a big garden, but it was a real mess. People only hired it for drinking and dance parties at the weekend. Mowing the lawn gave me pleasure from the fresh aroma of the newly cut grass. I enjoyed working alongside David, and the reward was that, after an hour, the garden looked beautiful.

"Do you know how to paint?" David asked next as we sat down and rested.

I had never painted a house before, so I hesitated. He didn't wait for an answer. "I need help to paint the hall and clean up the floor next Saturday so we can have the first meeting the next day."

I agreed, although I truly did not know what to do. Nonetheless, I went along and worked with him the next Saturday, and when we had finished, the hall was quite presentable.

The reward was immense on that first Sunday service in our new venue. I could see more people than ever, many with no Christian background, coming into the service. I realized that we would need a few more chairs for the visitors so that everyone could sit, but I didn't feel confident to take the initiative to get them until I was asked. After that first week I was put in charge of setting out chairs and didn't need to be asked anymore. I was pleased to be trusted to look after this basic need.

Because the church had become a family for me, I was learning that everyone was there for me to enjoy, to protect and to function alongside. We had mutual interests and were there to share our mutual joys, mutual pains, and, no doubt, mutual annoyances with each other. As my trust in God grew, His healing enabled me to interact more with the people in this community of faith. As with my family in Vietnam, I now had a true spiritual home of rest.

Early on at the scout hall I didn't see any ushers, so I volunteered to greet people at the door. I found myself enjoying it and welcomed new visitors with happiness in my heart. It came naturally, spontaneously from the life of Christ in me. I was not pretending. Visitors in turn appreciated a warm heart drawing them in. Seeing a young man at the door with a broad smile and joy in his heart affected them. The positive responses of believers who came to the service regularly also helped my confidence.

I found the work much more empowering and fulfilling than the drinking parties of my previous life. I was working with God to build up the body of Christ, and I sensed the Holy Spirit consistently pouring in His love and gifts.

The new church lacked funding, and soon I realized that as a member of the family I had a duty to contribute. At a drinking party my money went down the sewer, but now I decided to put it to better use. "Why not put the money you used to spend on alcohol and parties in the offering bag?" I asked myself. When I started doing this, an amazing thing happened: I found I could save more money than before, and my life improved overall. I had never dreamed that I would enjoy such a trajectory—from lost to found, from bad to good, and now from good to better every day. God had led me into a more satisfying life, and I would not go back to the old messy days again.

I never forgot to give thanks to the Lord God before I went to bed. This thankfulness helped me sleep better. I never regretted making a commitment to follow God and serve Him.

A couple of months after we moved to the scout hall, three Vietnamese families began attending the services. They didn't speak much English, so I volunteered to translate for them. God had trained me as an interpreter in Phanat Nikhom, and now, in Australia, He used me again. This increased my volunteer work, which I truly enjoyed. I was not so much a translator as a speaker, grasping the central idea of the sermon and conveying it to my people in their own language. It was a big challenge! But by nature I liked to contend with the unknown.

The work was worthwhile in itself, but for me the most amazing thing to come out of it was how my translating enriched me personally. From being sleepy in the service I was now giving the sermons maximum attention and finding them extremely helpful. I soon had a personal request for David.

"David, I want your sermon in writing," I told him.

He looked surprised. "What for?"

"I need to know your ideas, your central point, and your

direction so that I can keep up with you when you're speaking. You don't speak just for me to translate, so it would be more effective for me to know your train of thought beforehand."

David saw my point and consented. He wrote down his sermons and handed them to me before each Sunday so I could meditate on them, prepare the Scripture verses, and visualize my people and how to speak the message. The Lord taught me to get hold of the meat and bones of the ideas underlying a sermon. I didn't realize it when I began, but this interpreting would eventually spearhead the setting up of translation systems for future multiracial church services.

After the Vietnamese families came people from Laos, Cambodia, Thailand, the Philippines, and East Timor, as well as Chinese from various Southeast Asian countries. God was moving quickly, and we needed to be sensitive and flexible enough to keep up. He gave Pastor David the wisdom to build up His house. We learned to ride with His Spirit and respond to diverse needs as they arose. God moved and we followed; it was just that simple, natural and spontaneous. And there was joy in the work.

Chapter twenty-five

PRISON MINISTRY

He who is true in a little, is true in much; he who is false in small things, is false in great. (Luke 16:10 BBE)

And so my faith grew. From being a lost sheep I had become an adopted son of God. I had been drafted into the community of faith. I had learnt to forgive and felt the joy of being able to do so. I had realized my identity and worth were now in Him. And I had learnt to serve from His love and had seen God empowering me.

The Lord saw my faith and gave me more to do. God opened more doors for my humble service. I felt He was dealing with me as He dealt with Jeremiah:

Call to me and I will answer you and tell you great and unsearchable things you do not know. (Jeremiah 33:3)

To me it was certainly a 'great and unsearchable' thing that God would lead me back into prison, but that is what happened. Prison ministry began not through planning, but rather through taking up an opportunity that God unexpectedly opened for me.

It came about through Lyn's work as an ESL (English as a Second Language) teacher. In June 1991, one of her students, a young Cambodian named Rick, was charged for his criminal activities and sentenced to a prison term. As a good teacher she had a heart for this radical youngster lost between the Khmer and Australian cultures. She wanted to visit him in prison but was unwilling to go by herself.

Since we were good friends, she spoke to me about it one Friday afternoon. "I want to go to Parramatta prison to visit a student. Do you want to come with me?"

Prison? No way! I thought. I'd had enough of prisons. What on earth would I do there? The last thing in the world I wanted was to visit someone in jail.

My mind was troubled for one simple reason: I was truly afraid that going to a prison might bring back my past. It had happened to me once before.

Lyn had taken me to visit a zoo one Saturday a few months after I arrived in Australia. I enjoyed seeing the kangaroos and other native animals, and everything was going fine—until I saw a yellow dingo chained by the neck, lying under a fig tree. It had a food container and a water tin. The scene was exactly like my imprisonment under the Khmer Rouge, and I was totally unprepared for the shock.

As the memories flooded back, the past became so vivid to me that the hairs on my back rose. A cold chill overtook me and goosebumps covered my body. I grabbed at the mesh fence and almost passed out. It wasn't the dingo I saw chained to the tree—it was me.

Lyn was sharp and picked it up straight away. "Uong, what's the matter with you? Aren't you feeling well?"

I pointed to the dingo and told her the scene gave me chills as if I was under a malaria attack. Thank God for her discernment and intelligence—we left immediately. During the whole journey home I couldn't say a single word.

Now she was asking me again to venture into a prison. Afraid the flashbacks would reoccur, I told her, "You can go by yourself and maybe next time I'll go with you!"

Lyn went ahead with that first visit alone, leaving me unsure about whether to accompany her on the second visit two weeks later. But by nature I am an adventurous person, and I also like to test things. The more I thought about it, the more I wondered what would happen if I *did* go. *If God is truly healing me and restoring my confidence, then why don't I go to the prison and see what happens?*

I made a decision and rang Lyn to confirm that I was ready to go with her.

It was the first time I had ever entered a prison building by choice. All my previous imprisonments were forced on me. From the moment the prison gate opened I was afraid, but this time my eyes were not blindfolded but open to see. The fearful moment passed quickly because the prison guards were neither Khmer Rouge nor Thai military. One guard even smiled at us and directed us gently. His kindness helped to put my mind at ease. I immediately felt that this Sydney prison and the Khmer Rouge camp were as far apart as heaven and hell. In this building a humane approach to prisoners was followed, while among the trees of the jungle the Khmer Rouge were barbaric.

The Lord was with me that day, and everything was okay. I had no flashbacks or stress; instead I found I could talk to the guys inside easily. The very thing that made me comfortable was that I had also been a prisoner. I could patiently listen to them. They also asked about my past, so I was free to talk with them about it, and free to compare the differences between my Khmer Rouge imprisonment and theirs.

Rick and a few others were Cambodian by birth but had been raised in Australia. They were shocked when they heard I was in Khmer Rouge captivity for so long and yet survived. They couldn't believe their ears. So many Cambodians perished at the hands of those butchers, let alone hated Vietnamese soldiers.

These guys liked to hear what I had gone through in the jungle and the Thai military prison. It soothed their own complaints. "In Australian prisons you have almost everything," I commented. "The food is good, and there's hardly any torture or abuse. You only lose your freedom, not your human rights."

But above all these youngsters wanted to hear about Jesus Christ and how His power had saved, healed, and transformed my life. God had allowed my experiences, and now He used them to help build a bridge to these young men. My imprisonment gave me empathy with them, and, along with Lyn, a sensitivity and wit that gave birth to a short but sweet prison ministry.

The ultimate joy came when Rick responded to the Gospel and accepted the Lord Jesus as his Savior. Salvation came to him right there in jail. It was my turn not to believe my ears when he asked, "What can I do to know Jesus more?" I was speechless, and it was Lyn who prayed for him.

On the way home that memorable day, I felt like I was on a ride to heaven. The joy was so meaningful, and I knew it would last far longer than the joy I felt when I was set free from prison. Every time my joy increased, my faith in the Lord became more solid, and he again empowered me by His Spirit to honor Him and His work in my life.

More joy came when Rick began to reach out to other prisoners, and many more also accepted the Lord and His salvation. Rick was a born leader and had found something real in his life that he couldn't help but share. I never realized that Lyn's invitation to visit the prison with her would become a launching pad for God's work. Weekend after weekend, we would visit different boys in prisons around Sydney, connections made through those who had already accepted the Lord. I could see the way God was leading, and as the ox following Christ, I was also being fed in all aspects of life.

Seeing these young lives transformed by the power of God was a real bonus for us. Pastor David, even though busy with full-time work commitments and the heavy load of a growing church, became involved in this ministry as well. God opened the door initially to reach Cambodian boys, and this directly tested my heart attitudes. Could I minister to these young men without holding back because of the past? I'm thankful I truly could. God saw that, and many others were brought our way.

The results were far reaching. One young Nepali Hindu drug trafficker became a Christian and matured quickly, even in prison. After finishing his sentence in 1994 he was deported to Nepal, became a pastor in his small village, and planted a church. I began to see God's glory in the work of His hands!

Chapter twenty-six

MARRIAGE AND BEYOND

A wife of noble character who can find? She is worth far more than rubies. (Proverbs 31:10)

By now the Lord God had gradually and successfully healed all the pain of my past and restored my life. He gave me a hint that I should move on and build a new relationship. I had grown as an individual and felt I could again entrust my life to someone else.

I had a deep respect for Lyn as a lady with high moral standards. She was easy looking, intelligent, and solid, and her heart was 100 percent with God. We became friends when I already had a fiancée, Lan, so even though I admired her, in my mind I wanted her to be just a good friend. I talked to her many times about Lan and kept a good distance between us. We had a long-standing, solid friendship and mutual respect. That was the best way for us to view each other rather than in terms of physical attraction.

The friendship flourished but remained pure. I was not the type to jump ship, and I truly wanted to remain loyal to Lan, and allow myself time to heal.

Since Lan had ended our engagement, I had not seriously considered anyone else. But God's hint prompted me. As a believer I desired that everything I did would honor Him. I wanted a lasting friendship and a good marriage, so I began to pray about my future.

As I prayed, I found my admiration for Lyn grew. I appreciated her down-to-earth practicality. She had a successful career as a teacher and yet chose to live simply. I found comfort from her, and no doubt the love of God in her began to affect me too.

As I observed her and prayed, my affection for her grew steadily and gained momentum. Romance? No, we didn't begin as boyfriend and girlfriend, and we had never been on romantic outings or dates. Ours was a very practical friendship; if we went anywhere together, it was to places like prison. I never imagined that a lady who began visiting me two years earlier could overtake my heart, but she did.

I remembered the first time I met her in the halfway house in Crows Nest, when I offered her a glass of coffee half filled with condensed milk. Now she had become a sweetener to my heart. I loved her.

However, before I could make it 'official' that she was my girlfriend, I had to resolve a battle raging in my heart and mind. "She's not Vietnamese, so would a marriage to her last? How would I cope with differences of culture, food, and lifestyle?" I often asked myself such heartfelt questions. I was a man of war, so could she cope with my ways of handling life, or the hurtful and painful past that might again engulf me unnecessarily and destroy us both? There were more questions than answers.

I also knew that Lyn was not like a typical Vietnamese girl who relies a lot on her husband. She was more independent and strong-willed, and had even left home to study and work in Japan when she was 19 years old. Knowing her as an individual, I had to ask myself whether I could cope with her strong character. I wondered whether it was true love or merely infatuation. I wasn't a naïve young man anymore, and I didn't want to waste time in a vain, romantic courtship. Besides, as a believer, I couldn't live now as I used to. I had to be able to present Christ as my Lord and Savior here on earth.

In the end, I found I just had to trust God and let the Gospel be the center of my life, rather than culture and differences, or even intellectual analysis. The bond between Lyn and me was more than just the two of us; the Spirit of God was also involved. At last I had come to terms with acknowledging her as my soul mate.

Then it came to proposing. I knew she loved me, but I wasn't the kind to propose romantically by kneeling down and asking for her hand in marriage. All I said one afternoon was, "When are we getting married?" To my relief she paid no attention to my unromantic clumsiness and replied simply, "It's up to you."

There was another issue I had to fight to overcome. How was I going to tell my father about all of the changes in the last two years? He was very cultured and very Vietnamese. It was a tough question. I had always respected him as a good father who, besides teaching us well, had raised us successfully despite the pain of joblessness and war. I had to try to communicate with him on a more intelligent and less emotional level.

I decided the easiest way was to write to him about my plans to marry a New Zealander, not a Vietnamese girl as he wished. It must have been a hard letter for my parents and relatives to receive. In the past Dad had advised me to marry a person of the same race so it would save future headaches and heartbreak. It was especially challenging for him because it meant one of his children was deciding to move beyond his sphere of influence.

When Dad received the letter, he replied by sending many letters back. Never before had he written so much to me. Of course, he tried to make me think further about the differences in race and culture between Lyn and me, and about how we could expect to have a happy future together. Once he even challenged me with the line, "Since you went to Australia, first you rejected ancestral worship as your religion and became a Christian. Then you left your Vietnamese girlfriend, and now you even want to marry a Western girl! What next?" He even accused me of being the culprit behind the break up with Lan. It was hard to know what to say.

Of course, I had to defend my position, my future wife and my decision. I loved and respected Dad as a scholar, but that didn't mean I had to let him arrange my marriage. I had been away from home for ten years and had lived a challenging life. I had made many decisions about life and death without asking his advice. Now God was my Father, and it was He who was showing me the way to live. I had confidence that my life with Lyn would flourish, not in my own strength or wisdom, but in Christ. The center of our marriage would not be in us—not in our cultures, our intellectual analysis, or our similarities and differences—but in Him. I wrote back to my father to explain both my Christian faith and my decision to marry a 'foreigner'.

Dad knew his son well. He'd raised his children to be very much like him, single-minded and not fickle in decision-making. Yet he only stopped writing after I challenged him with a hard question: "Are all Vietnamese couples happy in their marriages?" Of course the answer was no. Even two people from the same race can face unhappiness in marriage. He never answered my question.

I was still young, but I had concluded that in this life I had two great blessings: the first, to know God, and the second, to marry Lyn.

Before our wedding I told her that she would have to manage the home with traditional family values. She would handle the finances in the family and I would hand her all my bankcards and the money I earned or saved. "However," I said, "there are two things you can't violate: I need pocket money for petrol and taking friends out for coffee, and I need to buy a book to read every week." I enjoyed gathering friends, both non-Christians and Christians, for talking and building friendships over coffee, and I also enjoyed reading great Christian writers.

Lyn, being a smart lady, agreed!

Through visiting prisons and sharing the Gospel with friends, the time came when I found I was being asked questions that I had no depth to answer. I couldn't rely on David for knowledge all the time—he also had a life to live, a family to care for and a growing church to shepherd. In any case, I didn't like relying on a secondary source of knowledge; after all, God was *my* Father too, and the Bible was *my* source of information.

I decided I needed to know the Author of my faith more deeply and to personally gain an understanding of sound teaching and doctrine so that I could nurture others well. I also wanted to learn from the experiences of the many great men and women who had walked with God before me. In short, I had a growing desire to study more formally.

Around this time there was a big conference in Sydney with speakers such as David Yonggi Cho, Bob Mumford and George

Otis, so I took a few days off work to go. While there, I took note of the Bible college that had organized the event. I'd never heard of Tabor College or its principal, Dr Barry Chant, but the contact encouraged me to step out and apply to study with them.

The study load was tough as I was doing full-time manual work and at the same time looking after our little family. My son, Tan Viet, was born, then a daughter, Linh Nhat Sara. It was very difficult coordinating study, work and family as well as being heavily involved in church activities and intermittent prison ministry. But I knew what perseverance was. After more than six years of part-time study, I completed my BA Ministry degree. My hope was to impart the joy and knowledge of the Lord God to my own people. This motivated me to the end.

Over 20 years have now passed since I first arrived in Australia. In that time God has done more 'great and unsearchable things' in my life than I can describe.

Six weeks after my marriage in 1992, I travelled back to Vietnam to keep my promise to my mother to return. At that time I was also able to make restitution to those I had hurt in my youth. I was chased and investigated by the local Communist leaders, who wanted to know why I was still alive when I was supposed to be dead. While there I dug up my own grave, erected for me by my family, and confronted the issue of shame in seeing my brother-in-law Ho, the military hero.

I've since been back to Vietnam with Lyn and our children a number of times. On visits in 2011 and 2012 I finally connected with most of the soldiers from my old unit. Between 1980 and 1986, up to 142 young men from my battalion were killed in action in Cambodia, and many were wounded as well. The others all settled back into civilian life in Vietnam. I worked with these old ex-servicemen to track down Dung Map and met him face-to-face after 29 years. I shook his hand and saw his wounded body. I discovered he was injured in that ambush and lost 41 percent of his physical capacity. The most important thing I did, however, was to offer him forgiveness.

I have also gone back to Cambodia to share the gospel and am involved in building up a number of churches in northwest

Cambodia, where my army unit was stationed. Returning to Cambodia for the first time was quite emotional for me. I often marvel at how God has taken me back to the very area where I almost lost my life. It has been a long journey—a journey of truly facing the past and not letting it impact me anymore; a long journey into freedom.

To this day, I wonder how I endured and survived such experiences as a jungle ambush and the hardships of captivity by the Khmer Rouge. I have no answers. One day, when my time on earth is done and I meet with God my Maker, the first question I will ask Him is: "Lord, how did I survive, and why?" All credit goes to God. It was He who sustained my life and allowed these things to happen so that I came to know and value life differently. Since I came to know Jesus Christ, both my life and the lives of others have held for me purpose and value.

When I was in Phanat Nikhom refugee camp, I met an American volunteer named Mike. I never knew his surname. Mike gave me a small English Bible, a New International Version. His timing was impeccable: this generous act made me aware that Protestant churches gave away Bibles, and soon afterwards I noticed the Vietnamese Bibles being offered by the Seventh Day Adventist Church. The Vietnamese Bibles were much bigger and the pages thicker than the NIV's, so they were more useful as wallpaper. I used some of the pages from Mike's Bible for rolling cigarettes instead.

On the day I read Ecclesiastes 11:9 and first thought about God's judgment, I stopped tearing up the little NIV. I kept it and brought it to Australia with me. Today it is one of my most treasured possessions from the camp. Many pages at the back are missing. I keep it in my glass cabinet and sometimes show it to the youngsters I reach out to as evidence of my arrogant days.

To me it speaks clearly of the guilt, fear and shame of my life without God. But it speaks even more loudly of His incredible mercy to me when I was completely lost—and His power to transform a life and make it a new creation.

Above left: New arrival in Panatnikhom Refugee Camp 1985; Inset: In the Camp with ex-soldiers in 1985; Below: Summer in the Camp, 1985

Left: Ex-soldiers in the psychiatric ward in the Camp

Below: Becoming an English teacher in early 1986

Top: Dung in the blue shirt, the photographer loaned me his camera;
Below left: Drunk; Inset: Celebrating Vietnamese New Year in camp

Above left & right: Looking for meaning in Buddhism; Below left: My first encounter with American nurse Rebecca Henry; Below right: After being rejected by the Canada delegation in 1987

Top: Parties like this often were enjoyed with dog meat; Above left: Searching for the truth. A Catholic church in the Camp, 1987; Above right: The girl that made us desire to wallpaper our home

Clockwise from top: The home with Bible wallpaper, Binh, 3rd right repatriated to Cambodia; The sign to the entrance of Panatnikhom Camp; The water jar that I had to fill every morning; Working with ARC (American Refugee Committee)

Clockwise from top: Refugee Camp, 1987; Refugee Camp, 1988;
Panatnikhom Camp, 1988

Clockwise from top left: My home in the Refugee Camp; Before departing to Australia, April 1989; Sydney 1989; With my sponsor Jenny in the Blue Mountains, 1989

Left: Japanese Garden in Auburn NSW, 1989

Below: Friends, ex-soldiers in Melbourne;

Clockwise from top left: At home in Cabramatta 1990; Lyn and I in the Blue Mountains, 1989; After marriage; In Melbourne Christmas 1989

Above: Lyn and I after we married; Below: Lyn, Ricky, Gam, myself and Tan Viet in Parklea Prison, 1994

Clockwise from top left: Parties with ex-soldiers in Sydney's West, 1990; With Jenny my sponsor at my Australian Citzenship Ceremony 1991; With my friend Hai in Melbourne

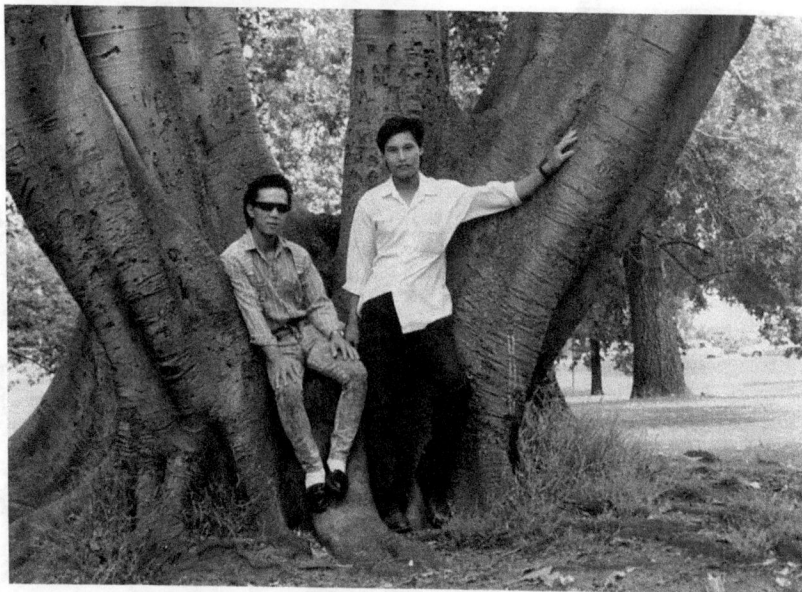